ELITE • 196

Napoleonic Light Cavalry Tactics

PHILIP HAYTHORNTHWAITE

ILLUSTRATED BY ADAM HOOK
Series editor Martin Windrow

First published in Great Britain in 2013 by Osprey Publishing,
Midland House, West Way, Botley, Oxford, OX2 0PH, UK
43-01 21st Street, Suite 220B, Long Island City, NY 11101, USA
E-mail: info@ospreypublishing.com

OSPREY PUBLISHING IS PART OF THE OSPREY GROUP

A CIP catalogue record for this book is available from the British Library

Print ISBN: 978 1 78096 102 6
PDF e-book ISBN: 978 1 78096 103 3
ePub e-book ISBN: 978 1 78096 104 0

Editor: Martin Windrow
Index by Marie-Pierre Evans
Typeset in Myriad Pro and Sabon
Originated by PDQ Media, Bungay, UK
Printed in China through Worldprint Ltd.

13 14 15 16 17   10 9 8 7 6 5 4 3 2 1

Osprey Publishing is supporting the Woodland Trust, the UK's leading
woodland conservation charity, by funding the dedication of trees.

www.ospreypublishing.com

EDITOR'S NOTE

Since a good deal of basic information applicable to both titles is given in
the companion volume, Elite 188, *Napoleonic Heavy Cavalry and Dragoon
Tactics*, several cross-references to that book are made in this text in order to
avoid lengthy repetitions. Readers wishing a fuller understanding of the
subject will find Elite 188 helpful.
Because this text includes material quoted from a wide range of historical
sources not all of which are specifically listed in the bibliography, the author
has provided a list of numbered source references; these will be found at
the end of the text, on page 63.

ARTIST'S NOTE

Readers may care to note that the original paintings from which the colour
plates in this book were prepared are available for private sale. All
reproduction copyright whatsoever is retained by the Publishers. All
enquiries should be addressed to:
Scorpio Paintings, 158 Mill Road, Hailsham, East Sussex BN27 2SH, UK
scorpiopaintings@btinternet.com
The Publishers regret that they can enter into no correspondence upon this
matter.

CONTENTS

NAPOLEONIC LIGHT CAVALRY TACTICS

INTRODUCTION: THE DEVELOPMENT OF LIGHT CAVALRY

According to Marshal Auguste Marmont, the conduct of war would have been simply impossible without light cavalry, which he described as the eyes and ears of the army, without which the general marched blindfold.

As explained in the companion volume Elite 188, *Napoleonic Heavy Cavalry and Dragoon Tactics*, in the 18th century there developed a type of cavalry somewhat heavier than the universal 'horse' of the earlier period, and at the same time another type notably lighter. Lightly armed cavalry on swift mounts had always existed, of course, and in a number of cases they employed the inherent skills of certain specific population groups. Sometimes these were not as regularly organized as 'line' cavalry – for example, the Spanish genetours, the Venetian stradiots and, most notably, the Hungarian hussars, who were among the first and most celebrated troops of this type.

Hussars were originally the light horsemen traditionally recruited from the Hungarian plains of the Austro-Hungarian empire. Their name was not, as is sometimes imagined, derived from the Hungarian *husz*, 'twenty' (from the notion that one man in every 20 families was conscripted), but from a Hungarian adaptation of the Italian *corsaro*, 'freebooter' – which is suggestive of their original status. The term came to be synonymous with expert horsemanship, élan and courage, and in time they were emulated in many European armies.

Initially such armies recruited what might be termed 'genuine' hussars, in an ethnic sense. In the French army, for example, the hussars recruited in the 17th century were of foreign origin, and one of their most famous regiments – Berchény – took its name from its first colonel, an officer of Hungarian background. Ladislas de Berchény had entered French service in 1712, and formed his regiment in 1720. (He was succeeded as colonel by his son and subsequently his grandson; the latter emigrated in 1792 during the Revolutionary 'Terror', and died in London in 1811.) A measure of the continuing 'foreign' nature of the French hussars is evident from the fact that at the conclusion of the Seven Years' War in 1763 almost three-quarters of the field officers and captains of the hussar regiments then existing bore foreign names. However, the origin of rank-and-file recruits was changing: until 1793 the Régiment de Berchény was recruited from Alsatians, and its language of command was German.

The archetypal hussar: *Général de division* Comte Antoine Charles Louis Lasalle (1775–1809), in his characteristically flamboyant uniform as worn in 1809. (The baggy riding overalls '*à la Lasalle*', presumably copied from the Mameluke *saroual* he had seen in Egypt, later became widely fashionable.) Baron de Marbot considered Lasalle the best of all light cavalry commanders, but complained that others tried to emulate his swashbuckling style without possessing his talent. Lasalle was given a brigade – the 5e and 7e Hussards – in February 1805; he commanded this '*Brigade Infernale*' ('Hellish Brigade') not just with brilliant dash, but with tight discipline and a close eye for detail, ensuring that men and horses were always ready for service at short notice. Lasalle had a mercurial temperament, often either elated or moody, and his passions were fighting, women, horses, alcohol and tobacco. The long pipe was a personal trademark, but the hussar officer Albert de Rocca recalled that most light horsemen smoked constantly, to while away their long hours in the saddle. (Print after François Flameng)

In Prussia, the first hussar regiment traced its origin to 1721, another to 1730, and a further six to 1740–43. One corps especially exemplified the practice of recruiting foreigners: what became the 9th Hussars originated as a company of 'Bosniaks' from Albania, transferring to Prussian service from that of Saxony, and in 1799 it became a corps of 'Towarczys' recruited from the gentry of Prussia's newly-acquired Polish provinces (see Men-at-Arms 485, *Polish Armies of the Partitions 1770–94*).

The experience of warfare in the early to mid 18th century demonstrated the value of light cavalry. Mounted on lighter horses, they could move more rapidly and with less fatigue than the heaviest cavalry, while in most cases they maintained the ability to fight on the battlefield in the same type of formations as the 'heavies' – albeit without the same potential impetus of the stirrup-to-stirrup charge. More importantly, however, the light cavalry were ideally suited for reconnaissance and skirmishing. They provided a screen behind which an army could advance or retreat without being observed by the enemy, and which could absorb any initial enemy thrusts. Their extra mobility was ideally suited for rapid advances or the pursuit of a beaten enemy, tasks that were virtually impossible for the heaviest class of cavalry. (There was, nonetheless, a blurring of the distinction in some armies: dragoons in particular could often act as effectively as the regiments designated officially as 'light' – see Elite 188.)

The characteristics of light cavalry service were described by a number of contemporary commentators, including Albert de Rocca, an officer of the French 2e Hussards (which even in the Napoleonic era continued to use, unofficially, its old name of 'Chamborant' – evidence of regimental *esprit de corps*). He summarized them as follows:

> The hussars and chasseurs were generally accused of being plunderers and prodigal, loving drink and fancying every fair thing while in the presence of the enemy. Accustomed, one may almost say, to sleep with an open eye, to have an ear always awake to the sound of the trumpet, to reconnoitre far in advance during a march, to trace the ambuscades of the enemy, to observe the slightest traces of their marches, to examine defiles, and to scan the plains with eagle sight, they could not fail to have acquired superior intelligence and habits of independence ... Forever smoking, to pass away his life, the light horseman, under his large cloak, braved in every country the rigour of the season.[1]

In a passage that has been quoted to emphasize the importance of training and discipline over skill-at-arms or élan, the Duke of Wellington described how he employed his cavalry. (His words are a mite ungenerous, since the British cavalry did achieve some noted successes in which their perceived want of order was not a factor.) Although Wellington does not refer here specifically to light cavalry, he rarely had much heavy cavalry under his command, and used regiments that were nominally 'heavy' for other tasks; certainly, his comments describe the essence of light cavalry service:

> My practice in regard to cavalry was this: first, to use them upon advanced guards, flanks, etc., as the quickest movers, and to enable me to know and see as much as possible in the shortest space of time; secondly, to use them in the momentary pursuit of beaten troops; thirdly, to use them in small bodies to attack small bodies of the enemy's cavalry. But I never attacked with them alone, always with infantry, and I considered our cavalry so inferior to the French from want of order, although I consider one squadron a match for two French squadrons, that I should not have liked to see four British squadrons opposed to four French; and, as the number increased, and order of course became more necessary, I was more unwilling to risk our cavalry without having a great superiority of numbers ... Mine would gallop, but could not preserve their order, and therefore I could not use them till our admirable infantry had moved the French cavalry from their ground.[2]

Hussars

It was said that light cavalry service demanded different attributes from those possessed by 'ordinary' cavalry. The noted French light cavalry officer Fortuné de Brack was certain that

> A man must be born a Light Cavalry soldier. No situation requires so many natural dispositions, an innate genius for war, as that of an officer of light troops. The qualities which render a man superior – intelligence, will, power – ought to be found united in him. Left constantly to himself, exposed to constant fighting, responsible not only for the troops under his command but also for those which he is protecting and scouting for, every minute finds employment for his mental and bodily faculties.[3]

Such a distinction could, perhaps, be taken to excess. A number of armies attempted to emulate the original Hungarian hussars not just in tactical employment but also in appearance: the braided jackets, fur-trimmed pelisses and fur caps that were characteristic of the original hussars spread to other armies, giving the hussar a swaggering air not just of confidence but also of showmanship (though one commentator remarked that it was not the pelisse that marked the hussar, but the man inside, and that their physical qualities and skill made the Hungarians the only true hussars).

Nevertheless, the 'typical' hussar attitude was exemplified by a remark of the great French hussar general Antoine Lasalle, who stated that any hussar who was not dead by the age of 30 was a blackguard (he himself outlived this limit, though not by much – he was killed at Wagram aged 34). Antoine de Marbot described a typical hussar of the old school as 'a hard drinker, a brawler, always ready for a quarrel and a fight; brave, moreover, to the point of rashness ... absolutely ignorant of everything that did not concern his horse, his accoutrements, or his service in the field ... a jolly ruffian [with] ... his shako over his ear, his sabre trailing, his florid countenance divided by an enormous scar, moustaches half a foot long, waxed and turned up to his ears, [and] a regular rowdy air'.[4]

A French hussar, *c.* 1795, displaying a typical period hairstyle with hanging plaits from the temples. Note the 'mirliton' headdress often worn by this branch in continental armies. This cylindrical cap with a cloth 'flame' wrapped around it was known in German as a *Flügelmütze* or 'winged cap'. Other features of traditional hussar dress seen here are the short dolman jacket lavishly corded across the breast, the hanging fur-trimmed pelisse overjacket similarly corded, the parti-coloured 'barrel sash' at the waist, and tight Hungarian-style breeches with embroidered 'knots' on the thighs. (Print after Hippolyte Bellangé)

Chasseurs and light dragoons

Appearance aside, the tactical attributes of such troops became so obvious that they spread to the more orthodox line cavalry, leading to the formation of light units such as those styled 'chasseurs' (hunters), until the light horse evolved from being a specialist addition to representing the largest part of an army's mounted force.

This was exemplified by the development of light cavalry in the British army. In April 1756 it was ordered that for reconnaissance and similar duties a troop of 'light dragoons' was to be added to each of 11 regiments of Dragoon Guards and Dragoons; their members were to be 'light, active young men' between 5ft 6½in and 5ft 8in tall, their mounts 'nimble road horses' not under 14 hands 3in, with saddles like those used by jockeys. Their arms were to be carbines 51in in length, with bayonet; a pistol; and a straight-bladed sword with a light rather than a 'basket' hilt.

A British light dragoon trooper, *c.* 1760, representing the development of light cavalry. His uniform is similar to that of the line regiments of 'Horse', apart from the distinctive high-combed cap, slung carbine, and lighter boots already characteristic of this branch of service.

The equivalent French arm of service were the Chasseurs à Cheval. This trooper of *c.* 1792–95 wears the early dark green braided dolman; the 8e Régiment, illustrated here, had rose-pink cuff facings. This type of crested helmet, known by the English name 'Tarleton', was worn between 1792 and 1796. (Print after Eugène Lami)

French Chasseur à Cheval wearing the shako introduced in c. 1805 and, again, the braided dolman in imitation of hussar uniform. This branch wore jackets and *habits* of several different styles before 1812. (Print by Martinet)

The uniform was to be like that of the parent regiment, but with a 'jockey-cap' headdress with a brass comb or crest instead of a cocked hat (presumably both for protection, and because the latter hampered the handling of the carbine), and they were to wear light jockey boots (presumably because they would not need the leg protection required for boot-to-boot charges in close order).

The experiment was so successful that the first entirely light regiment was raised in 1759 – the 15th Light Dragoons – and not only were subsequent newly raised regiments all given this designation, but some of the existing Dragoon regiments were converted to Light Dragoons. (Although elements of hussar dress were adopted by some light dragoon units, it was not until 1806–07 that four British regiments were officially styled and equipped as Hussars.)

Chasseur c. 1812, now wearing a short-tailed 'Kinski' or *habit-veste*. The rolled cloak provided considerable protection against sword-cuts, and so common was this practice that the order to roll cloaks came to signify the imminence of action. (Print after Hippolyte Bellangé)

Expansion

The utility of light cavalry became so obvious that they came to outnumber the heavy regiments. For example, at the end of the Napoleonic Wars the British army included 15 regiments nominally 'heavy' and 19 of Light Dragoons. At the height of Napoleon's power in 1812 his army (including the Imperial Guard) maintained 17 heavy regiments (plus the Gendarmerie d'Élite of the Guard), 25 of dragoons, but 52 light regiments, the latter thus representing about 62 per cent of the whole cavalry arm. The comparative value of the light arm might be suggested by the fact that when the nine regiments of Chevau-Légers-Lanciers (lancers) were created in 1811, three were converted from existing light regiments but the other six from dragoon regiments. Such proportions were replicated in many armies. The Prussian army might appear to have been an exception in that in 1814, for instance, their regular cavalry comprised four cuirassier and six dragoon regiments, to only six of hussars and four of Uhlans (lancers); but all the Landwehr (militia), National and Freikorps cavalry could also be classified as 'light'.

Some light cavalry units were created to perform a specific role, as in the case of the French Chevau-Légers-Lanciers, formed with the intention that they would be attached to the higher formations of heavy cavalry to provide these corps with a scouting and skirmishing facility for which the heavy regiments were unsuited. Another variety of French light cavalry formed for a specific purpose were the three regiments of Éclaireurs raised in December 1813 as part of Napoleon's Imperial Guard, their name being indicative of their intended role as 'scouts' (*éclairer* means both 'to illuminate' and 'to reconnoitre'), during what was inevitably going to be a defensive campaign on French soil the following year. The 1st Regiment counted as part of the Grenadiers à Cheval and the 2nd of the Dragons de la Garde, but the 'scouts' were not intended exclusively to provide a light element for heavy regiments; the 3e Éclaireurs were part of the Chevau-Légers-Lanciers Polonais de la Garde, and wore their uniform. In the event the Scouts, deployed as individual squadrons, also fulfilled the same purpose serving with line as well as Guard units.

Trooper of the French 2e Régiment des Éclaireurs de la Garde Impériale; although not specified in the original orders for the raising of the Scouts, lances were carried. Affiliated to the Dragons de la Garde, this regiment wore a green uniform with crimson facings, and a crimson '*shako rouleau*' in the style worn by hussars late in the First Empire. The fact that the Gardes d'Honneur and the three regiments of Scouts of the Guard were raised for the 1813–14 campaigns, instead of new heavy corps, underlines the relative importance that Napoleon attached to his light cavalry. (Print after Eugène Lami)

ORGANIZATION & DEPLOYMENT

Unit strength

As described in the companion title on heavy cavalry (Elite 188, to which the reader is referred for much of the basic information), the organization of units was fairly similar in most armies. The principal formation was the regiment, comprising a number of squadrons each of two 'troops' or 'companies', the squadron being a primary manoeuvre element. The number of squadrons in a regiment varied, but four was fairly standard for service in the field. Although regimental establishments were sometimes greater, even those with five or more squadrons often left one or more behind when a regiment went on campaign, to act as a depot for the training and supply of reinforcements.

In the case of the British army, for example, in general regimental establishments were increased from eight to ten troops in December 1805 (excluding the regiments serving in India, and the 1st Dragoon Guards, which traditionally maintained one more squadron than the norm), but one squadron was generally left at home. In late 1813 the four hussar regiments were increased to six squadrons each, but at the end of the war all regiments reverted to four squadrons.

Attrition on campaign could lead not only to a (sometimes severe) diminution in the numbers of mounted men in each troop, but sometimes to reorganization. In the Peninsula in October 1811 cavalry regiments were reduced to three squadrons, two troops being sent home; this presumably involved the withdrawal of cadres, with most rank-and-file being distributed among the remaining squadrons to bring them nearer to establishment strength. Establishments were not

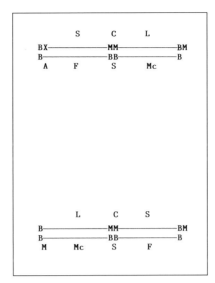

French light cavalry squadron in *colonne par divisions* (front at top). Each of the two companies is in two close ranks, with a frontage of about 24 metres; a gap of about the same distance between the companies gave the second company freedom to manoeuvre without disordering the first. Officers and NCOs are indicated by letters, troopers by lines, though the precise order might vary according to strength.
Key: C = *capitaines*;
L = *lieutenants*;
S = *sous-lieutenants*;
Mc = *maréchaux-des-logis-chef* (sergeant-majors);
M = *maréchaux-des-logis* (sergeants); X = *maréchal-des-logis* with standard (if carried);
B = *brigadiers* (corporals);
F = *fourriers* (quartermaster-corporals); A = *adjutant-major* (warrant officer).

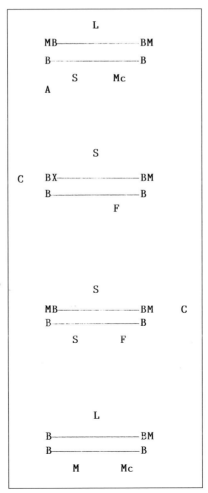

French squadron in *colonne des pelotons* – i.e. drawn up in separated half-companies. Each half-company platoon is in two ranks, with half the frontage of the column-of-divisions, and with manoeuvring gaps between platoons equal to their frontage.
Key as previous diagram; here the two company-captains ride on opposite flanks of the central half-companies.

A regiment of French Chasseurs à Cheval on the march, showing a typical column of two or three files abreast. The leading element is the regimental *compagnie d'élite*, recognizable by their red-plumed fur caps; the officers in the lead have the white plume identifying field and staff officers. (Print after H. Chartier)

always uniform within the structure of an army; in 1806, for example, while most Prussian heavy and dragoon regiments had five squadrons each, the ten hussar regiments (including the Bosniak Regiment), plus two of dragoons, each had ten squadrons. There was also often an increase in the numbers of men in a squadron for active service when compared to peacetime establishments.

Even before attrition began to take its toll, on campaign units might already be considerably weaker than the official establishment. An example is provided by the light cavalry of Napoleon's Armée du Nord in 1815. According to the establishments of the previous year, each regiment would comprise four squadrons of two companies each, each company 78 strong (4 officers) with 63 horses; with the addition of regimental staff, this provided a minimum of more than 500 mounted men. At the beginning of the campaign the regiments with the field army (most with four squadrons, but some with three) had an actual strength of only 410 of all ranks, and when the three strongest regiments are excluded the average strength of the remainder was only 366.

Deployment

The manner in which the light cavalry regiments might be deployed in the field depended to a considerable extent on the numbers available. Armies with a relatively small force of cavalry might have the light horse organized administratively in brigades and divisions, as part of a single cavalry command, with brigades or individual regiments allocated to accompany particular infantry formations as required. This, for example, was the case of the British cavalry in the Peninsular War, where there was no official, permanent attachment of cavalry contingents to larger formations.

Where more cavalry was available, they could be deployed as what was sometimes styled 'corps cavalry', with some brigades, regiments or even squadrons attached to particular *corps d'armée* or lesser formations, while others were organized into divisions or corps of 'reserve cavalry' not attached to any infantry formation. The concept of a *corps d'armée* as a self-contained miniature army required an integral cavalry force to perform its reconnaissance and escort duties, and to support the infantry and artillery on the battlefield, for which duty light cavalry was almost always employed. The heavy regiments, whose primary function was to act as a striking-force on the battlefield, were often concentrated in formations of 'reserve' cavalry, to which a small number of light regiments might be attached to perform those duties for which the 'heavies' were unsuited.

General Joseph Rogniat, a distinguished French engineer and writer on tactics, stated that while the heavy cavalry should be concentrated in large formations in the rear of the line of battle, the light cavalry should be kept on the flanks – both of the heavy regiments, and of the army in general – specifically to pursue an enemy broken by the charge of the heavies, and not to make the first charge themselves. This was especially necessary, he wrote, to permit the heavies to rally after their own charge, so that often the light cavalry in effect formed a second wave after the heavies had performed their task.

British hussar trumpeters. It was specified that orders should be given verbally in a loud voice, and in some cases accompanied by gestures with the sword. It is reasonable to wonder what effect signal-calls blown by trumpeters could actually have had once a unit was launched upon a charge, until the time came for their very necessary task of sounding the call to 'rally'. Nevertheless, although they were regarded as an addition to, not a substitute for verbal orders, it was still important for the troopers to be familiar with the regulation calls. In the British service there were ten of these: March; Trot; Gallop; Charge; Halt; Retreat; Rally; Send Out Skirmishers; Skirmishers Cease Fire; and Call In Skirmishers.

Three examples of the international spread of hussar uniform styles. (From left to right:) Russian hussar officer, c. 1812; Spanish hussar regiment 'Maria Luisa' (although this is a contemporary image, this unit normally wore a red dolman with its light blue pelisse and breeches); and officer of British 10th Light Dragoons (Hussars), c. 1812. (All prints by Goddard & Booth)

A FRENCH REGIMENT IN COLUMN

This plate provides a visual impression of the amount of ground taken up by a regiment of French Chasseurs à Cheval, drawn up in column with a frontage of about 50 metres. Regimental strength was established in 1807 at four squadrons, each of two companies (i.e. in British terms, troops), each company 128 strong with four officers. In fact, on campaign the actual unit strength was often very much lower; here we show squadrons with only about half their establishment, as might be the case late in a hard-fought campaigning season. In this configuration the two companies of each squadron are drawn up side by side – when in a column-of-divisions, the depth would be double that and the frontage halved.

The regimental commander (RC), with his assistant (A) and a trumpeter (T), waits for orders in front of the first squadron. Each squadron is assembled in two ranks of about 50 men, the ranks a horse-length apart; additional NCOs (N) form a 'serrefile' rank about two horse-lengths behind the rear of each squadron. An additional NCO rides on each flank of the front rank of each squadron to help maintain order. Squadron junior officers (O) ride about the same distance in front of each front rank; the captain squadron commander (SC) and his trumpeter are centred two horse-lengths in front of them, and the second, junior captain (2C) – commanding the second of the squadron's two companies – behind the serrefile rank. The distance between squadrons is here about 25 metres, sufficient to permit a company to manoeuvre to the flank without disordering the remainder.

(Inset) A factor in command-and-control was the trumpeter, whose task in battle was to transmit by trumpet-call the orders of his officer. Traditionally trumpeters wore a more elaborate uniform than that of the other rankers, often in 'reversed colours' (i.e. with the body of the coat in the regimental facing-colour); this, together with their grey horses, made them easily identifiable in action by the officers. The trumpeter shown belongs to the French 7e Chasseurs à Cheval, c. 1809, a regiment that served at Wagram that year, and subsequently in the Peninsula and the 1812 Russian campaign; their facing colour was rose-pink. In French service 'reversed colours' were replaced officially for all units by green uniforms with 'imperial' lace according to regulations of December 1811.

It is puzzling that the diagrams of formations in many period manuals either omit to specify the positions of trumpeters at all (e.g. the British manuals), or place them together at some distance from the officers (e.g. the Prussian diagrams). The same is generally true of company drummers in infantry manuals. We might speculate that the manuals illustrate the manoeuvres specified for the exercise-field, and that it was not felt necessary to actually illustrate the fact that in action trumpeters and drummers were to attach themselves to the relevant officers to pass their orders.

The cut against infantry, from the British *Rules and Regulations for the Sword Exercise of Cavalry* (1796). This was one of the few occasions when it was thought safe to deliver a blow with a bent arm, to achieve maximum force without being vulnerable to a cut in return.

MOUNTS

As noted in Elite 188, the mounts of light and heavy cavalry were not always as different as theory might suggest, although it is true that the light regiments usually had smaller, lighter and more agile mounts than the largest horses suitable for cuirassiers. Ideal light-cavalry mounts were usually less expensive to purchase, easier to source, and cheaper to maintain than the heaviest horses, and were more suited for prolonged operations.

Marbot stated that it was insufficient to separate the cavalry into light and heavy by the nature of their horses. He concurred with the obvious view that the heaviest, armoured troopers needed the largest, strongest horses, and that the light cavalry needed nimbler horses for long, rapid movements, reconnaissance and advance guards. But he also stated that an intermediate mount was required, retaining some qualities of the heavier mounts, which presumably implied that individual light cavalry regiments should have been allocated specific duties according to the quality of their horses. This did, in fact, occur, for example in the size of mounts specific to various formations in the French army, at least in theory, though under active-service conditions it was not always possible to maintain the desired standard of remounts.

As light cavalry might be constantly on the move when on campaign, training of and care for their mounts were paramount for their effective employment. De Rocca stated that 'the rider and his horse, accustomed to live together, contracted a character of semblance. The rider derived animation from his horse, and the horse from his rider ... during a march, the horse would gently slacken his pace, or lean on one side or the other, to keep his intoxicated and sleeping master in the saddle; and [the hussar] would go without his own bread to feed his companion'.[5] The latter was apparently no exaggeration. David Roberts of the British 51st Foot recalled the difference between British and German troopers: 'A German Soldier will sell his Bread to feed his Horse – A British Soldier will sell the [horse's] Corn to purchase Drink'.[6] George Gleig of the British 85th concurred: 'the horses of the foreigners were ... in far better order than those of our countrymen ... an Englishman ... never acquires that attachment to his horse which a German trooper experiences. The latter dreams not under any circumstances of attending to his own comfort till after he has provided for the comfort of his steed. He will frequently sleep beside it, through choice; and the noble animal seldom fails to return the affection of his master, whose voice he knows, and whom he will generally follow like a dog'.[7] Such concern for the welfare of mounts was of especial significance in light cavalry, who might be ranging ahead of the army for prolonged periods, away from a ready supply of remounts.

EQUIPMENT

Light cavalry equipment was in many ways similar to that of the heavy cavalry, though with a marked difference in the common design of sabre and its mode of use. Straight-bladed sabres as carried by most heavy cavalry were designed for the thrust or for a downwards chopping blow; but for light cavalry, more likely to participate in individual combats requiring more dexterity, sabres were generally curved, designed for a slash or cut.

The precise techniques employed depended upon the nature of the enemy: against cavalry, ideally the cut was delivered with a straight arm, movement coming from shoulder and wrist, to minimize the danger from an opponent's blow; but against infantry it was better to cut with a bent elbow to exert maximum force. The point of a curved sabre could also be used, as noted in the British *Rules and Regulations for the Sword Exercise of Cavalry* (1796): 'the point should seldom or never be given in the attack, but principally confined to the pursuit, when it can be applied with effect and without risk. The case is different in acting against infantry, as the persons against whom you direct the *point* are so much below your level, that the weight of your sword is not so felt; consequently it is managed with greater facility than with an extended arm carried above the shoulder ... against infantry, the point may be used with as much effect as the edge and with the same degree of security'.

Furthermore, charging with the sabre levelled at the height of an infantryman could deliver a thrust with force increased by the impetus of the moving horse. Examples of the use of the light cavalry sabre against infantry are illustrated in Plate B.

Firearms formed a much more important part of the light trooper's equipment than they did for heavy cavalry, the heaviest of which were unsuited for the skirmishing for which firearms were principally used. All light cavalry carried saddle-pistols, and most carbines, the employment

Bavarian cavalry, *c.* 1806: a dragoon (left), in a white uniform faced with red, and a chevauxleger (the contemporary German spelling) in green. In a general 'lightening' of the Bavarian cavalry comparable to practice in several other armies, Cuirassier and Dragoon regiments were converted to Chevauxlegers between 1799 and 1811. This crested leather *Raupenhelm* (lit., 'caterpillar helmet') was worn in a number of German armies; in the Bavarian service it replaced an earlier style called the '*Rumford Kasket*'. (Print after Rozat de Mandres)

of which is covered below (see 'Skirmishing', and Plates G and H). The other light cavalry weapon, never used by the heavy cavalry, was the lance (see below, 'Lancers', and Plate F).

The light cavalry's defensive equipment was appropriately much lighter than that of the heaviest cavalry, since it was unsuitable for light horsemen to be loaded with cuirasses or metal helmets, and the high boots used by some heavy cavalry were not necessary for the light as they were less likely to make boot-to-boot charges. Light cavalry headgear was not necessarily less protective than that of the 'heavies', however; indeed, some commentators advocated a strong leather shako as being preferable to a metal helmet, not just because it was less fatiguing to wear but because it afforded as good protection. This was also true of the fur-crested leather 'Tarleton' helmet, despite its being prone to warp out of shape on campaign.

More elaborate light cavalry headdress could prove less effective: the tall cloth mirliton cap, for example, was not as robust as some others, and some fur colpacks (busbies) favoured by hussars could offer little protection. In 1809 Robert Ker Porter stated that 'Most of our brave fellows who felt the edge of the French sword were cut in the head; and that owing to the little defence which the present form of their caps allows ... the flimsy, muff-like appendages that encumber the heads of so many of our soldiers. Indeed, this awkward cap of ours, by being constructed partly of paste-board, soaks up a great quantity of wet during the violent rains of this country, and becomes so heavy and disagreeable, while it affords no protection to the wearer. At all times they can be cut down to his skull with the greatest ease'.[8] The fur hussar caps were replaced in some British regiments (e.g. the 7th and 10th) by more robust shakos that gave greater protection.

B | **USE OF THE SABRE AGAINST INFANTRY: VILLERS-EN-CAUCHIES, 24 APRIL 1794**

For an example of the use of the curved light cavalry sabre against infantry, we show figures of British 15th Light Dragoons from one of the most noted cavalry exploits of the early Revolutionary Wars (until 1911 this British battle-honour was spelled 'Villiers-en-Couche', and one of the earliest published accounts actually styled it 'the Affair of Landrecies').

The Allied commander, the Austrian LtGen Otto, was reconnoitering with his vanguard – two squadrons of Austrian hussars (who have been variously identified), and two of the 15th Light Dragoons under Capt Robert Pocklington. Encountering a large force of French cavalry, Otto intended to await the arrival of his main body, but on receiving news that the Emperor Francis II was in the vicinity and in danger from the French cavalry he decided on an immediate attack. As the Allied squadrons charged, the French cavalry drew aside to reveal a mass of French infantry and artillery; but the charge went on, overran the guns and smashed into the infantry, when horses brought down by their musket-fire broke the French formation. The 15th retained their order, rode through the infantry, routed the French cavalry as it tried to re-form, galloped on and cut up an approaching siege-train, and, after a 4-mile ride, only stopped when they came under fire from the French garrison of Bouchain.

Unsurprisingly, their horses were by now 'blown', but Capt Pocklington calmly re-formed and retraced his steps at a trot, despite the proximity of French troops (who may not have recognized his command as British because of their blue uniforms); it seems that Pocklington formed a rearguard of skirmishers to discourage pursuit. Returning to the original battlefield, Pocklington found his escape barred by the French infantry through which he had charged. By now they had been rallied and perhaps even reinforced, but they had apparently been so shaken by their earlier experience that when he charged them again they failed to stand, and the light dragoons broke through to safety. From the total Allied force of 272 – about two-thirds British – the Austrians suffered 31 casualties, and the 15th Light Dragoons 17 dead and 17 wounded; French losses were estimated at about 1,200 and three guns.

Austria decorated the British officers involved in this astonishing exploit, and their cooperation was commemorated by the Austrian pattern of lace worn subsequently by the 15th Hussars. Above all, this engagement demonstrated what could be achieved when discipline was maintained even after a furious mêlée.

(1) & (2) The cut delivered with the elbow bent, while passing an opponent on foot.
(3) The thrust against an opponent on foot. The elbow is locked and the blade is pointed and held flat, with the cutting edge outwards.

FORMATIONS & TACTICS

Although skill with the sword was perhaps more necessary for the light cavalry than the heavy, with the 'lights' more likely to engage in open-order combat than the close formation of a 'heavy' charge allowed, discipline and the ability to retain formation were still of paramount importance. The fact that these outweighed individual skill-at-arms was observed by Napoleon when considering the merits of his own troops and those of the Mamelukes encountered in Egypt in 1798–1801. He stated that whereas two Mamelukes could out-fight three Frenchman, 300 French would overcome the same number of Mamelukes, and 1,000 French would defeat 1,500 Mamelukes.

Even troops regarded as fully trained might disappoint in some aspects, as reported of six British regiments by the *Morning Chronicle* on 5 September 1798:

> ... confessedly the elite of the British Cavalry; and if men, horses, and discipline be considered collectively, it is probable that the world cannot match them. A defect, however, with which our horse is often reproached by foreigners still exists. They are not well broke to fire. When feux de joye were fired on the birth days of the Prince of Wales and Duke of York, a great number of horses were so scared by the report of the pistols, as to run out of the ranks, in spite of all the efforts of their riders.

The experience gained from campaigning was also a vital factor in the effectiveness of cavalry; as Lasalle once remarked to de Brack, 'War is to the soldier who has never been out of his garrison, what the world is to a young man leaving school: what practice is to precept'.

In most cases the formations used by light cavalry were like those of the heavy, as described in Elite 188. Most manuals and manoeuvre regulations made little distinction between the types of cavalry, although some parts were more applicable to one type than the other (notably, skirmishing). Comments made at the time suggest that some official manuals may have seemed unduly complicated, and – as was apparently often the case with the infantry – it is likely that on campaign the number of manoeuvres might be reduced to a practical minimum, with the more complicated evolutions reserved for the

A troop of cavalry changes position, by a common method of 'filing'. A line of two ranks moves into a column two abreast, the front and rear men in each file riding side by side, then form a two-rank line again, facing in the opposite direction. In the original position (left) the ranks are in 'close order', in the new position (right) they are up to a horse-length apart; in British practice this spacing was sometimes styled simply 'order'.

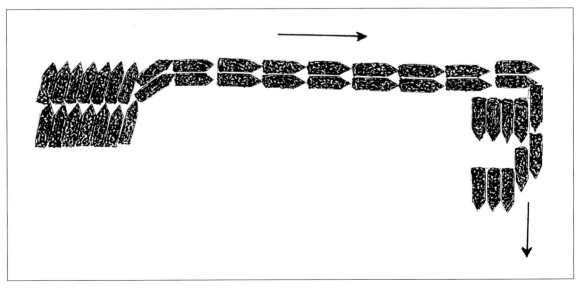

parade ground. Variations must have been adopted based upon the experience of campaigning, as described by tactical writers like de Brack; some aspects of light cavalry work were in any case not covered in detail by the regulations, so *ad hoc* practices must have been introduced.

As an example of how the basics of light cavalry service could be reduced to a minimum, the manual issued in 1794 for the South Holland Squadron of Lincolnshire Yeomanry – i.e. troops with only limited time for training – consisted of only 15 pages, with information stated in the plainest manner. For example: 'close order' was when the rear rank was as near the front rank as possible without touching the front horse's tail; 'order' was when the gap was one horse-length between ranks; and 'open order' when the gap was half the troop-frontage. Similarly, 'close files' was when boot-tops were touching, and 'half-open files' when the trooper's outstretched arm was just able to touch his neighbour's coat collar.

An indication that the more complicated manoeuvres were not generally required on campaign may be provided by a field day of four light and three heavy British regiments in the Peninsula in June 1812, conducted by Stapleton Cotton: 'Sir Stapleton put them through some movements, contrary to the desire of Lord Wellington, who said he had no wish of the kind. After doing one or two things, the affair got confused, the Peer rode off in the midst of it, expressing what he thought, "What the devil is he about now?"'[9]

A rare eyewitness depiction of cavalry in the field: Bruyères' 1st Light Cavalry Division of Eugène de Beauharnais' IV Corps of the Grande Armée near Ostrovno, 25 July 1812. The unit in the centre is in line, in the usual two ranks; in the right background another advances in column. (Print after Albrecht Adam)

A front rank of British light dragoons charging. The uniform in this contemporary print is that of the mid 1790s, and the sabres are held 'pointed' rather than in the 'guard' position. The 1788 light cavalry sabre had a less curved blade than the 1796 model, and thus was easier to 'point'.

The charge

Again as described in Elite 188, manoeuvre was generally performed in column, and while columns could be used for combat it was more common to attack in line. The number of ranks in a linear formation was the subject of discussion at the time, some advocating that three ranks provided additional 'weight' to the impetus of a charge, though Marbot stated that the third rank inhibited rapidity. Generally a two-rank line came to be

BRITISH REGIMENT DEPLOYING FROM COLUMN INTO LINE, UPON A CENTRAL TROOP

These schematics represent a British light dragoon regiment of four squadrons, deploying from a column-of-troops into a line based on Troop 4. (A similar manoeuvre could be carried out based upon one of the flanking troops – see Elite 188, *Napoleonic Heavy Cavalry and Dragoon Tactics*, Plate D.)

(1) The initial column, commonly used for manoeuvre, consists of the eight numbered troops (two per squadron) one behind the other.

At the word of command, the three leading troops wheel to the right, and ride in column-of-twos at right-angles to the initial column until Troop 1 reaches the intended position for the right flank of the line. They then wheel left, and Troops 2 and 3 advance into alignment with Troop 1, leaving a gap between the flanks of the 1st and 2nd Squadrons (i.e. between Troops 2 and 3).

(2) The regulation movement for a troop wheeling to the right from a two-deep line, here in close order, and filing off in a column-of-march.

(3) Troop 4 then marches forward to take up its position in the new line. The following troops wheel to the left and march in column-of-twos until they are parallel to and behind their places in the new line, whereupon they wheel right in

succession and advance into alignment.

(4) The prescribed method of wheeling (or 'filing') to the right from column-of-march into line, to form two ranks.

(5) The normal formation of a British cavalry squadron when the unit was in column-of-troops – each troop in two ranks (here, each of say 25 troopers and NCOs, stirrup to stirrup) one behind the other. The squadron commander **(SC)** is positioned a horse-length in front of the centre of the front rank; two senior NCOs **(N)** form *serrefiles* two horse-lengths behind the front troop, and two more plus one of the junior officers **(O)** two horse-lengths behind the second troop. The gap between troops in column-of-troops is not specified in the regulations, but was presumably about three horse-lengths.

(Inset) This depicts a Prussian skirmisher using a pistol in the absence of a carbine; note that by regulation the drawn sabre is suspended from the wrist, which must have rendered the pistol – never accurate at the best of times – even less efficient. In the 1813–14 campaigns it was the Prussian practice to attach a squadron of volunteer mounted Jägers to a cavalry regiment, to provide an enhanced skirmishing capability. The uniform shown is that of the 4th Hussars (1st Silesian), in which the Jägers wore a green *Litewka* instead of the usual hussar dress, with the regimental facing colour on the collar.

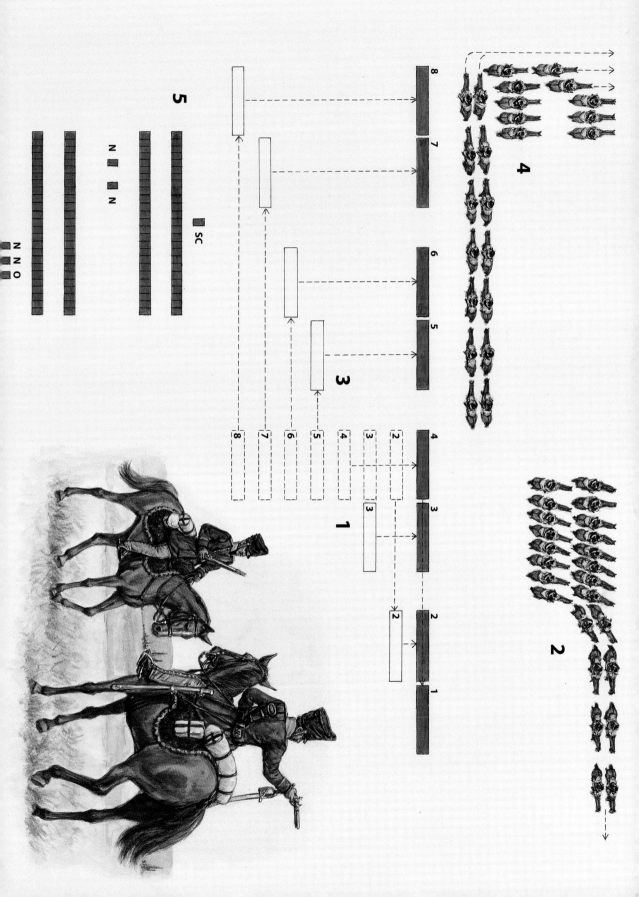

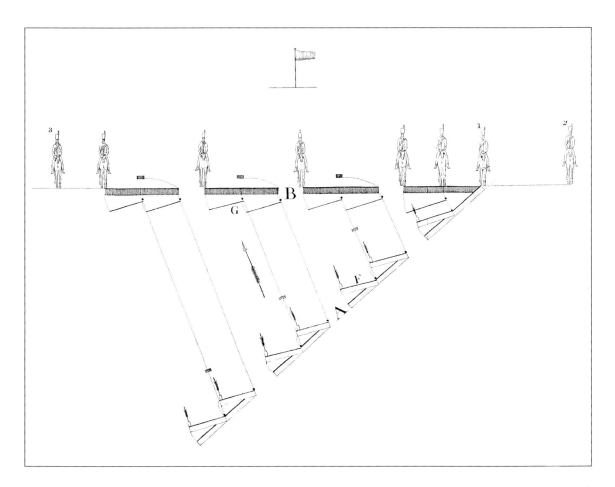

A British regiment of four squadrons changes its facing from position A to position B. Each troop (half-squadron) manoeuvres individually, wheeling on its right flank as a pivot (F); then it advances, and wheels again (G) to take up the new line. In the new line the soldiers designated (1), (2) & (3) are 'markers', who ride ahead to indicate the new position.

preferred, though a compromise was advocated by a writer in the *British Military Library or Journal* (1798), who stated that a third rank could be employed with effect providing that it was no more than ten paces behind the second rank, and as the charge came near to contact the third-rank men should move into the intervals in the first two ranks, so that in effect the three-rank line became two. It is possible that the common mode of the light cavalry charge might have provided more intervals in the first two ranks than the closely-packed charge '*en muraille*' (lit., like a wall) conducted by the heaviest cavalry.

The merging of a third rank into those preceding it during a charge was in fact the common practice of the '*serrefile*' NCOs and officers who rode behind the second rank. It was stated at the time that their presence in the rear was vital to prevent men from dropping back deliberately to escape the first clash, and that similarly NCOs or officers at the end of each rank would prevent men from straying – a vice to which those on the flanks were more prone than those in the centre, the latter being kept steady by the men each side of them.

Although the light cavalry might charge in a slightly looser formation than the classic 'heavy' charge, its mechanics were much as described in Elite 188. Important factors included the progressive increase in speed so that the charge impacted upon the enemy at maximum velocity, and the ability to maintain formation, including the maintenance of manoeuvre-gaps between squadrons, so that upon repulse the leading element could swerve around those following and not disorder the remainder by riding into them.

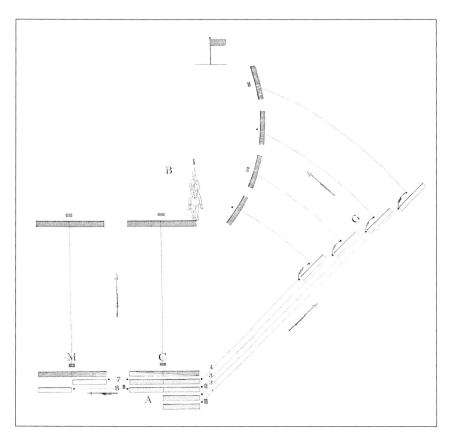

A simultaneous attack on the front and flank of an enemy force (B). From the column of squadrons (A), one squadron deploys to the left (M). Two others file to the right to position (G); they then wheel left, to attack the enemy's flank. Meanwhile the left squadrons, (M) & (C), charge the enemy's front.

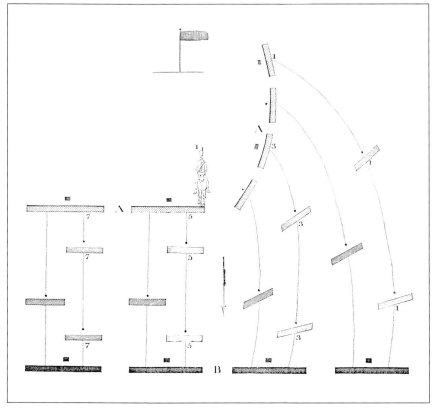

A regiment of four squadrons retires by troops from the L-shaped deployment at position (A) to a new line at position (B). The right-hand troop of each squadron – numbered (1), (3), (5) & (7) – retires for a distance, then halts and faces front, to cover the withdrawal of the left-hand troops. These then halt in their turn, and cover the renewed withdrawal of the right-hand troops, and this leap-frogging manoeuvre continues until the whole regiment reaches the final position.

French hussars charge, led by the squadron commander with his trumpeter in close attendance. Although not contemporary, this splendidly spirited image does give an impression of a light-cavalry charge, somewhat different from the often slower, knee-to-knee attack employed by some heavy cavalry. (Print after Edouard Detaille)

Commenting largely on light cavalry, de Brack advocated that swords should only be drawn towards the end of an advance: keeping them sheathed, he stated, might confuse the enemy about the reason for the forward movement, while the flashing of the blades when suddenly drawn at relatively close range could unnerve them, just as it put heart into those charging.

D

A CHARGE IN ECHELON

This plate depicts a regiment of four squadrons of French hussars advancing on the enemy in echelon, a common tactic that was recommended especially when engaging infantry.

The component squadrons advanced in 'echelon' or staggered line, each generally in line formation (though the manoeuvre could also be carried out by a unit in column), so as to permit each squadron to come into action successively. Its value against infantry was that it was calculated that the leading squadron would receive the enemy's fire and the next might fall upon them before they had time to reload; or, that if the infantry fired by platoons, then the first two squadrons would absorb the musketry, shielding those following. Sufficient lateral manoeuvring distance was left between the flanks of successive squadrons so that one might retire to re-form without disordering those following. Because the squadrons advanced in a staggered formation, each would have an approach to the enemy unencumbered by casualties from the preceding wave, or by troopers turning back to escape the enemy's fire.

Because it was important that each squadron arrived at its target riding at maximum speed, the elements of an echelon attack might be moving at different rates at the same moment. Thus, here the rearmost or fourth squadron **(4, and inset 1)** is still moving at a walk, in the formation illustrated on Plate A. About 150m in front of them, the third squadron **(3)** is at a trot. The same distance in front again, the second squadron **(2)** is working up to a gallop, with the *serrefiles* moving up into the second rank. Meanwhile the leading squadron **(1, and inset 2)** have got to within about 100m of the target – an Austrian infantry square. They are at full gallop, and the *serrefiles* have pushed their way in among the second rank of troopers. The formation is beginning to waver, as some horses pull ahead, others veer towards the flanks, and the first enemy volley causes casualties.

The echelon attack could also be employed against cavalry. In that case the second and succeeding squadrons could provide decisive impetus into the mêlée created by the collision of the leading squadron with the enemy, or could target a different part of the enemy formation – flanks, as always, being the most vulnerable.

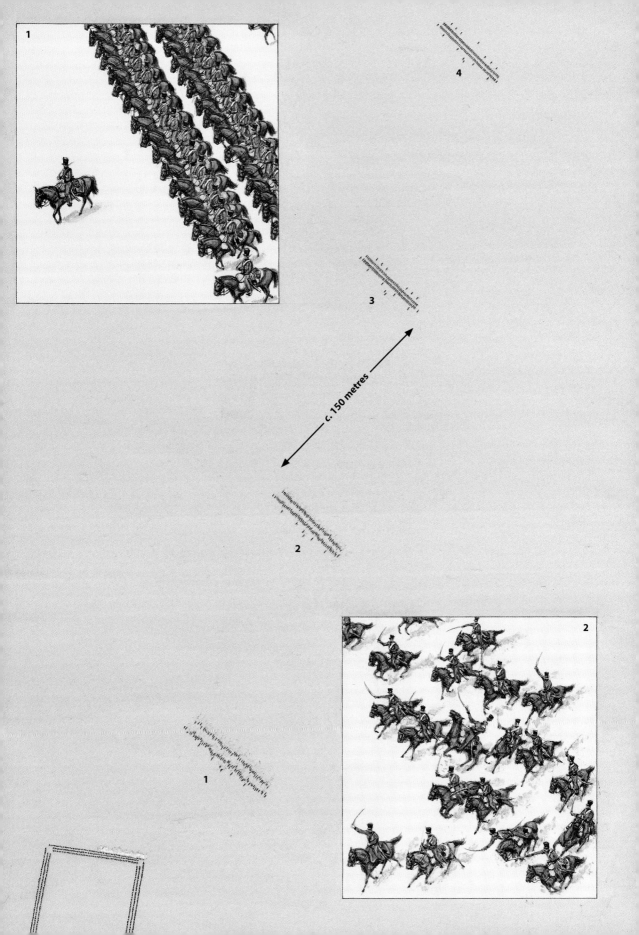

c. 150 metres

The rally

As with heavy cavalry, the ability to rally after a mêlée was of crucial importance, so as to be able to resist a countercharge, as well as to maximize a renewed advance by continuing to ride in formed ranks. It was recommended that when rallying a formation should move forward slowly, since it was easier to control horses at a gentle pace than when having them join a halted unit. It was also advocated that officers attempting to rally their men after a charge should gallop to the position of those furthest forward in the pursuit of the enemy and give the signal to rally, so that the rest would rejoin the ranks as they continued to ride forward and came up with those furthest in advance. It was observed that it was easier to rally defeated light cavalry than heavy, since the speed of the former's mounts could rapidly take them a sufficient distance for the rally to be effected before a victorious enemy, moving in formation, would have time to come up – under which circumstances the Prussian cavalryman Emanuel von Warnery stated that the victors might as well pursue a flock of sparrows. He believed that any attempt to rally a defeated unit nearer to the pursuing enemy would be futile, for though all involved would cry 'halt!', none would cease to run until out of immediate danger.

Aspects of manoeuvre and charges are illustrated in the colour plates. With heavy cavalry often held back as a central reserve, the position of light cavalry on the wings served the dual purpose of protecting the army – they were sometimes thrown out in skirmish order a considerable distance away to warn of, and impede the attack of, enemy flank-attacks – and (at least according to de Brack) of disquieting the enemy by their very presence and their ability to mount a rapid attack. The additional mobility of light cavalry theoretically permitted them to be transferred rapidly along the army's front if required.

Light versus heavy cavalry

It was believed that light cavalry would be at a distinct disadvantage if they engaged heavy cavalry, the weight of the 'heavies' being capable of overthrowing the light by impetus and intimidation. There were occasions when light horse seem to have avoided such contact deliberately; for example, it was noted at Eckmühl in April 1809 that the light cavalry of both sides were engaged against each other when the contending armies both sent cuirassiers forward. In Marbot's version of the action, the light cavalry 'drew off promptly to the flank, to avoid being crushed by these formidable steel-clad masses, who advanced rapidly upon each other, met with a shock, penetrated each other, and became one immense mêlée'.

One solution to the problem of engaging heavy cavalry was for the light horse to attack in column and endeavour to penetrate the heavy formation, bringing about man-to-man combats in which the 'lights' might not be at such a disadvantage. In single combat a light cavalryman, in theory more manoeuvrable than one riding a larger mount, might have an advantage even over an opponent protected by armour. Edward Cotton recounted an engagement at Waterloo between a member of the 3rd Hussars of the King's German Legion and a French cuirassier:

> The hussar was without a cap, and bleeding from a wound in the head, but that did not hinder him from attacking his steel-clad adversary. He soon proved that the strength of cavalry consists in good horsemanship, and not in being clad in heavy defensive armour. The superiority of the hussar was visible the moment the swords crossed: after a few wheels a

tremendous facer made the Frenchman reel in his saddle, and all his attempts to escape his more active foe became unavailing; a second blow stretched him on the ground, amidst the cheers of the light horseman's comrades.[10]

Another tactic when confronting an advance of heavy cavalry in line was advocated by de Brack: to divide into two wings – in the case of a regiment of four squadrons, into bodies of two squadrons each – and move rapidly to right and left respectively, leaving a gap into which the heavy cavalry might advance. Each wing could then turn inwards and fall upon the enemy's flanks before the 'heavies' had time to change their formation. It was claimed that this manoeuvre was even more successful if a second line following the first continued to move straight on, occupying the attention of the enemy and making him even more vulnerable to the flank-attacks by the first line.

An attack on the enemy's flank was always the tactic

that potentially offered the best chance of success. De Brack described how, even when attacking in line, he had formed one of his flank squadrons into column and sent it to threaten to turn the enemy's flank; even if it did not succeed, this would divert the enemy's attention and unsettle his line.

There were certainly occasions when light cavalry defeated heavy. Marbot recalled how at Wagram in July 1809 there was a singular meeting of regiments on opposite sides which possessed the same *Inhaber*; Prince Albert of Saxe-Teschen was colonel-in-chief of both these units, one of Austrian cuirassiers and one of Saxon hussars. 'Impelled by duty and the point of honour', presumably arising from their close connection, they charged each other, and Marbot recorded the universal surprise when the hussars defeated the 'heavies'. He believed that they must have been anxious to expunge the stain occasioned by the recent defeat of Saxon infantry.

However, protracted cavalry encounters in which both sides remained firm were rare. For example, a writer in the *United Service Journal* in 1831 claimed that 'Nobody but Dundas [under whose aegis the British regulations were formulated] ever supposed the possibility of two lines of cavalry coming in positive and simultaneous contact; one or other must either give way, turn about, and fly, or else, falling into disorder, be penetrated and passed through, so as to produce a complete mêlée, in which that party which first regains any degree of order will have the instant advantage'. William Tomkinson, a very experienced light cavalry officer, concurred; writing of an action before Fuentes de Oñoro, he commented that 'This is the only instance I ever met with of two bodies of cavalry coming in opposition, and both standing, as invariably, as I have observed it, one or the other runs away'.[11]

Immobility under fire

One factor effecting deployment on the battlefield was the consideration that cavalry might have to remain immobile for long periods. Whereas the 'heavies' might be stationed towards the rear until the time came for them to act, light cavalry might be posted nearer the battle line, and even within the enemy's gun-range. Under such circumstances, tactical writers recommended that commanders shelter their troops behind features in the terrain, such as undulating ground, to protect them from the worst of the enemy fire, and have them dismount. This might seem obvious, but it was sometimes ignored; for example, at Borodino in September 1812 it was remarked that much of Napoleon's cavalry stood under fire for protracted periods, sustaining casualties most of the time.

While advocating the tactic of sheltering men, de Brack also remarked that it was not always a bad thing to expose a unit to enemy fire for a short period prior to an advance, as troops who had suffered losses would charge with greater determination, partially from a desire for revenge and also because they would realize that charging was potentially less dangerous than standing still to be shot down one by one.

E **THE 'SCHWARM' ATTACK**

A tactic used by some German armies was sometimes described as the *Schwarm* ('swarm'), or 'attack on flanks and rear'; it was most often employed against infantry, and, at least in Prussian service, it could combine both heavy and light cavalry. Since they were mounted on lighter horses, it was thought at one time that hussars were not suited for the main line of battle, so they might be shielded until the most opportune moment for their deployment.

This schematic treatment shows a dragoon regiment of five squadrons (**D**) – standard for the Prussian army before the reorganizations following the war of 1806 – plus six squadrons of hussars (**H**). The heavier dragoons are assembled with all five squadrons in line. Drawn up behind their flanking squadrons are two columns each of three hussar squadrons, with a half-squadron frontage; sufficient manoeuvring distance is left between them, and between the hussars and the dragoon line. In advancing into the attack the hussars were concealed, and thus shielded from enemy fire. When they got within charging distance the hussar squadrons would wheel out beyond the flanks of the dragoons and rush upon the flanks and rear of the enemy, surprising them without having to suffer incoming fire during the approach. A variation of this tactic involved the main body of cavalry being shielded by a strong force of skirmishers, who would advance and fire upon the enemy before the main line charged.

(**Inset**) One of the light cavalry's most significant duties was scouting and reconnaissance. The troopers shown are Prussian *Landwehr*, the force best described as a form of militia raised for the Wars of Liberation in 1813–14, which greatly expanded the size of the Prussian army. This branch of service comprised both infantry and cavalry; the latter were exclusively light horse, generally armed with lances, and wearing a fairly simple uniform including the *Litewka* frock-coat and a shako. The distinguishing badge of the whole force was the 'Landwehr cross', in shape like that of the Iron Cross decoration. The establishment of the mounted *Landwehr* as light cavalry emphasized both the importance of that arm and the fact that they were easier to mount and equip than heavier regiments.

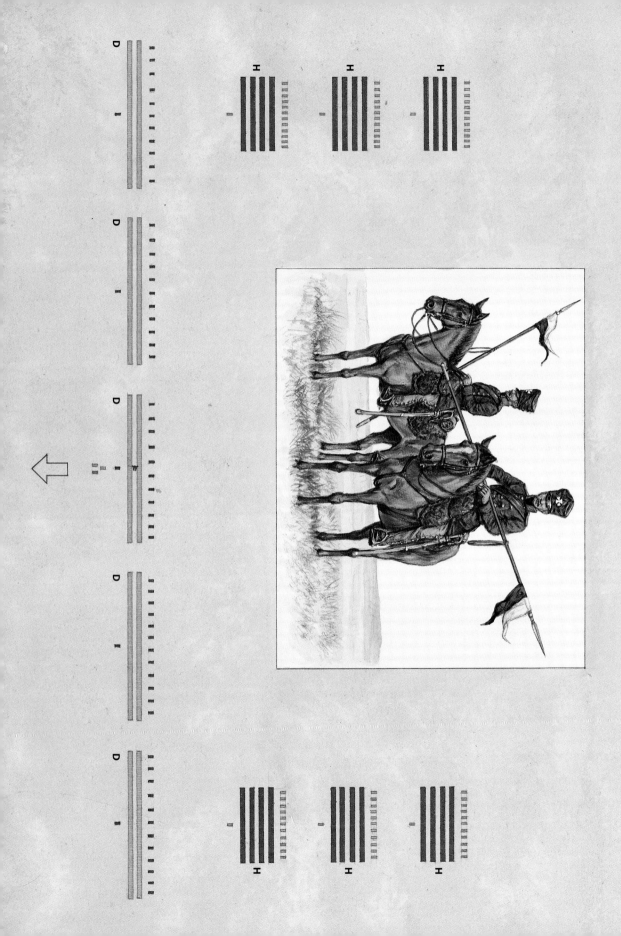

The co-ordination of light cavalry and mobile artillery: French hussars attempt a disputed river crossing at Dierhoff, 18 April 1797, supported by artillery that has kept pace with the cavalry advance. (Print after Coignet & Girardet)

CAVALRY & HORSE ARTILLERY

The concept of cavalry acting in unison with artillery was perhaps especially relevant in the case of the light cavalry. The advent of rapidly moving horse artillery capable of keeping pace with cavalry presented the possibility of providing them with immediate fire-support. In armies that possessed sufficient cavalry to be organized into their own larger formations, it was common for horse artillery units to be permanently attached to specific cavalry formations. In Napoleon's Grande Armée at the outset of the Russian campaign of 1812, the four corps of 'reserve cavalry' had integral horse artillery batteries either attached to specific divisions or forming a corps reserve. The same applied to the Armée du Nord in 1815, in which the four cavalry corps had companies drawn from the 1er – 4e Régiments d'Artillerie à Cheval attached, one company per division. Such artillery could support both heavy and light regiments, and was especially useful for 'softening up' squares prior to cavalry attacks, since infantry in such tightly packed formations were especially vulnerable to artillery fire. Had French cavalry and horse artillery been better co-ordinated at Waterloo, for example, the outcome might have been different.

In the early stages of the French Revolutionary and Napoleonic Wars the concept of close artillery support had led to regiments maintaining their own artillery, integral to the unit; in the infantry these were sometimes styled 'battalion guns'. However, they fell out of use when it became obvious that they could hinder the rapid movement of a regiment in return for only a limited fire effect (though the system was resurrected by Napoleon in 1811). In the cavalry such guns could usually keep pace, and there were examples of cavalry regiments maintaining their own fieldpieces; in British service these were sometimes styled 'curricle guns' or 'gallopers'. They were used, for example, by light dragoons in the Netherlands campaign of 1793–95, and on occasion in subsequent years. The successful relief of the besieged survivors of the Vellore mutiny in 1806 was due in part to the fact that the relief force of the 19th Light Dragoons had their own two 'galloper guns' which they used to blow in the gates of the city.

When charging against artillery some tactics were fairly obvious, such as using folds in the terrain to keep the cavalry as sheltered as possible before launching a charge; attempting to take artillery in the flank; and keeping enemy infantry between the artillery and the route of approach for as long as possible so as to restrict the guns' field of fire. De Brack recommended that bodies of skirmishers should precede an advance on artillery, whose fire against them would be relatively ineffective due to their scattered deployment, while they could screen the approach of the main body.

LANCERS

Light cavalry armed with lances formed a distinct element of mounted formations, involving some specific tactical practices. Because of the nature of the weapon, and the training required to produce a proficient lancer, it had generally fallen from use by the mid 17th century. Its later employment was originally associated with nations for whom it was a traditional weapon – notably, Poland and adjoining regions (hence items of uniform that came to be associated with lancers had their origin in Polish national styles, especially the *czapka* or 'lancer cap'). In Poland itself lancers formed the greatest part of the cavalry; of the 20 cavalry regiments of the Duchy of Warsaw, for example, no fewer than 14 were lancer corps (15, if the 21st Lancers is included – a regiment formed in Lithuania in 1812, though it is doubtful that it ever reached establishment).

Many of the original lancer corps in other armies also had their origins in troops for whom the lance was a traditional weapon. In Austria, for example, the Emperor Joseph II ordered the creation of a *'pulk'* of light cavalry armed with lances after

Austrian Uhlans, *c*. 1812–14. These troopers are acting as scouts, perhaps for heavier cavalry following them, and advance with wide gaps between the files. Note the square-topped Polish-style *czapka* headgear. The partition of Poland between Russia, Prussia and Austria after 1795 gave all three powers recruiting access to communities for whom the lance was a traditional weapon. (Print after R. von Ottenfeld)

One of the more unusual light cavalry units of Napoleon's Imperial Guard was the Lithuanian Tartars, a Muslim squadron raised in 1812 by a Polish army officer, LtCol Mustapha Achmatowicz, and attached as scouts to the short-lived Lithuanian 3e Régiment de Chevau-Légers de la Garde. That regiment was wiped out at Slonim in October, but surviving Tartars were incorporated into the Polish Lancers, and fought throughout the 1813 German campaign. This watercolour shows a trooper skirmishing with a pistol; the style of his uniform and his small mount are reminiscent of the Cossacks that the squadron faced in 1812.

the acquisition of Polish territory, and in 1791 the existing 'divisions' of lancers were united into a regiment. Initially they were organized in Polish style, with the flank divisions (*Flügeldivision*) armed with lances and the remainder with carbines, thus combining the capacity for conventional attack with skirmishing. Similarly, the Russian army had no lancer regiments as such until 1803, when the existing 'Light Horse' (Polish and Lithuanian Tartars) were converted to that role, thus exploiting their indigenous skills. Prussia maintained a unit of 'Bosniaken' from 1745; originally a squadron of lancers raised in the Ukraine for Saxon service, this was attached to Frederick the Great's 5th Hussars, eventually attaining regimental strength and being allocated the number '9' in the list of hussar regiments. In 1799 the Bosniaks were disbanded and replaced by a corps of *Towarczys* ('comrades') raised in the Polish territory acquired by Prussia; these formed the basis of the first Prussian lancer regiments titled as such (*Uhlans*).

 LANCERS IN ACTION

Although the lance was thought by some commentators to be ineffective if a mounted opponent could deflect its thrust and get inside its reach with the handier sabre, it was lethal against infantry unless they were in square, and it had one advantage even against that formation. Even in very wet weather, when the rain made muskets inoperable, a steady square could still remain largely invulnerable to conventionally armed cavalry by virtue of its hedge of bayonets. Under such conditions, however, lancers could ride up without any risk of being shot, and stab at the infantry while remaining out of bayonet-range.

Marbot recalled how at Katzbach in August 1813 his 23e and 24e Chasseurs à Cheval confronted a Prussian square that was unable to fire because of the rain, but all the chasseurs could do was cut ineffectively at the musket barrels: 'The position on both sides was truly ridiculous; we looked each other in the eyes, unable to do any damage, our swords being too short to reach the enemy, and their muskets refusing to go off.' Then the 6e Chevau-Légers-Lanciers were sent up in support. Their lances outreached the bayonets and stabbed a pathway through the infantry, into which the chasseurs

rushed and routed them, while 'the sonorous voice of Colonel Perquit could be heard shouting, in a rich Alsatian accent, *"Bointez, lanciers, bointez"*. [13]

A similar incident is recorded at Dresden in the same month, when Austrian infantry held off French cuirassiers until Gen Latour Maubourg, commanding I Cavalry Corps, ordered up his escort of 50 lancers; these troopers stabbed a breach in the Austrian formation, to permit the cuirassiers to burst in amongst them. (This incident was quoted by Marmont in support of his assertion that a proportion of all types of cavalry should be armed with lances – not a view that attracted wide support.) De Brack recorded a more uncommon use of the lance against an impenetrable square at Waterloo, when one of his men hurled his lance like a javelin; but although it hit one of the infantrymen, no gap was opened.

Here, the rider in the foreground is shown stabbing overhand with his lance at Austrian infantry in close order, while the trooper in the right background demonstrates the commonest grip, with the lance 'couched' under his right arm. Note that the pennon was usually unfurled when charging, in the belief that its fluttering might upset any enemy horses whose riders might be engaged.

A later artist's impression of the Lancers of the Vistula Legion overrunning Colborne's Brigade at Albuera in May 1811. While inaccurate in details, it does give an impression of the vulnerability of infantry to lancers if they were caught in line or column formation. On this occasion the cavalry burst into view over the brow of rolling downland, under cover of a rainstorm and gun smoke; they caught most of the brigade before it had time to form square, and effectively destroyed three regiments.

Advantages and handicaps

There were conflicting opinions concerning the merits of the lance. Marmont, for one, stated that because Cossacks and similar troops were adept with the lance some theorists regarded it as a natural weapon for light cavalry. However, it was his view that it had only been adopted originally by Cossacks out of necessity, since it was easy and cheap to manufacture, and it should actually have been regarded as the weapon of heavy cavalry, as it had been in the early 17th century. He advocated its use by the front rank of all cavalry, believing that in the charge lances would penetrate the enemy's line, at which point the second rank could follow and use their sabres.

One of the disadvantages of the lance was the time needed to master its use, and the most proficient lancers were found only among those peoples who had used it since boyhood. The Cossacks are usually quoted as an example in this regard, but they were not alone – as testified by Henry King of the British 5th Foot, who in 1810 observed the guerrillas of Don Julian Sanchez: 'I examined one of their pikes [sic], which was a very light handy weapon. These men, having all been bull-fighters, manage them with wonderful skill and adroitness; and, a few days before, one of them had thrust this formidable weapon through one, and wounded another, of the enemy, in his rear'.[12] The need for extensive training was exemplified by a report concerning the French 3e Hussards when issued with lances as an experiment in 1800–01, when it was observed that they were not so much 'armed' as merely 'carrying poles'. Similarly, some difficulties were encountered when Prussian Landwehr cavalry received lances from 1813. Conversely, when Russian hussars were issued with lances before the 1812 campaign it was noted that they soon became sufficiently adept to be effective against skirmishers, and also that their morale improved through the belief that the lance gave them an advantage.

Against infantry the lance could be an instrument of pure execution, as exemplified to dreadful effect by the slaughter of Colborne's Brigade by the Polish 1st Lancers of the Vistula Legion at Albuera in May 1811. When they burst upon the infantry out of the concealment of rolling terrain and under the cover of a rainstorm, the casualties they inflicted exemplified the devastating nature of an attack by light cavalry moving so rapidly that infantry had no time to react and form square. It is difficult to be precise, because some casualties among the four infantry battalions had apparently been inflicted earlier by artillery fire, and, conversely, because the numbers stated to have been present may have included baggage-guards who were not actually engaged, which would have affected the percentage rate of casualties. Nevertheless, the statistics are compelling.

The first battalion hit by the French 2e Hussards and 1er Lanciers de la Vistule was the 1st Battalion, 3rd Foot, which lost more than 85 per cent in killed, wounded and missing (the latter mostly captured). The next in line was the 2/48th, which lost almost 76 per cent, and the third battalion, the 2/66th, lost some 62 per cent. The fourth, furthest from the initial impact, was the 2/31st; this battalion was attacked after the French cavalry had lost impetus and had become disorganized, so it was able to form square and drive them off – but it still lost 37 per cent of its strength. (Even against a steady square the lance offered an advantage over the sabre – see Plate F.)

Lancers had an especial advantage during the pursuit of infantry, in that they could stab men lying down to escape the reach of sabres – a tactic whose legitimacy was debated. William Leeke, who fought at Waterloo, expressed one viewpoint: 'I trust no British soldier will ever use the lance as the French used them at Waterloo, for the purpose of putting the wounded to death… War is dreadful enough as it is, but how much more terrible would it be, if no quarter was to be given to those who should fall into the power of their opponents; and yet to this state of things the employment of Lancers evidently tends'. [14] Conversely, it was not unknown for infantry to throw themselves flat and allow enemy cavalry to ride over them (in the knowledge that horses will avoid treading on a man if possible), and then to stand up and re-form. One such incident occurred at Jena in October 1806: having rallied after a charge, the French 7e Chasseurs à Cheval took a different route back from the path of their advance, because the Prussians over whom they had ridden had got to their feet and were again in formation. (Under such circumstances, the spearing of men lying down might have been considered justified.)

Against cavalry, however, the lance was often held to be less effective, although there were conflicting opinions concerning single combat or general mêlée. A British writer in the *United Service Journal* in 1831, quoting experience of the Napoleonic Wars, stated that 'A bad lancer is a much more clumsy fellow than a bad swordsman; not only is his weapon by far the most difficult to manage, but his powers of horsemanship are materially affected by his awkwardness in attempting to wield it'. Nevertheless, the writer claimed that 'a single lancer on a very well-broke horse, is more than a match for a single swordsman, supposing them both expert at their respective arms', for

there is hardly any horse that could be brought again to face the lancer, or even prevented from turning short round, and completely exposing his own rider to his attack, when once it has received upon the nose one of those tremendous blows which can be given with the staff of

French Chevau-Léger-Lancier. Although the uniform details in this early depiction are dubious (the cowhide helmet-turban is missing, and the lance-pennon is shown quartered), it does illustrate well the common method of 'couching' the lance under the right arm for the charge. A narrow strap wound around it at the point of grip could be used either to secure it to the wrist, or, when unwound, as a sling around the shoulder when the rider needed both hands free. (Print by Debucourt after Carl Vernet)

the lance by swinging it round with the whole strength of the arm, and by means of which men who are good masters of the weapon will actually strike a man clean off his horse if they get a fair stroke at him in this manner.[15]

De Brack concurred, stating that such a 'wave' with the lance could be effective even if only to knock the enemy off-balance, using the forearm rather than the weight of the whole body so as not to compromise the lancer's seat. Even the lance-pennon had a tactical implication, as remarked by the British officer Thomas Dyneley: 'When our dragoons make a stand to receive them, the flags [pennons] frighten the horses, and they go about and the lancers have them through the body in the "twinkling of an eye"'.

Lancers were also effective as long as their formations remained rigid, when levelled lances could present an impenetrable barrier (as in the example quoted in Elite 188, pages 12–13, when at Genappe on 17 June 1815 French lancers blocked a street so that their opponents were unable to close with them). De Brack recalled how at Maloyaroslavets in October 1812 two outnumbered squadrons of lancers kept themselves safe by almost forming a square, lances levelled front and rear, so that a huge force of Cossacks was too intimidated to engage.

The unwieldy nature of the lance was, however, a serious inconvenience if the point were turned. Marbot recalled an incident at Polotsk when his 23e Chasseurs à Cheval charged Russian Guard Cossacks, who initially held them off with lances 'held very straight ... but when, at length, my troopers had pierced the bristling line of steel, all the advantage was on our side. In a cavalry fight the length of lances is a drawback when their bearers have lost their order and are pressed closely by adversaries armed with swords they can handle easily, while the lancers find it difficult to present the point of their poles. So the Cossacks were constrained to show their backs, and then my troopers did great execution'.[16] (Marbot's last remark also reminds us of the fact that in a cavalry combat most casualties were caused after one side had broken and turned).

Other writers concurred with Marbot. For example, William Tomkinson wrote of an incident in the Peninsula in 1811 in which 'The Lancers looked well and formidable before they were broken and closed to by our men, and then their lances were an encumbrance... We had only one person ... hurt with a lance, and when retiring, they got on the ground, caught in the appointments of other men, and pulled more dragoons off their horses than anything else'.[17] Similarly, William Swabey wrote that 'a body of [lancers] makes a very pretty tournament appearance... They owe their reputation to having destroyed a great many of our infantry when their ranks were broken at Albuera, but as to their being formidable to formed troops it is quite ridiculous; a dragoon with his broadsword is worth two of them'.[18] A writer in the *United Service Journal* in 1834, commenting on the action at Genappe, stated that 'the long unwieldy two-handed lance, at all times ridiculous on horseback, is totally useless the moment you close with the gewgaw champion who bears it' (the lance was, of course, generally used one-handed).

The disadvantages of the lance became so obvious that Napoleon came to restrict its use even in the Imperial Guard, which included the two most famous of all the French lancer corps (the Polish, and the Dutch or 'Red' Lancers): from April 1813, only the front rank carried the lance, with sabre and pistol, the second rank and all corporals carrying instead a sabre, pistol, carbine and bayonet. De Brack remarked on the advantages of carbine-armed light cavalry when opposing lancers; he advocated they be attacked in column, as was done against heavy cavalry, so as to penetrate their formation. When once you had got among them, the lancers, 'closely wedged, can neither parry nor point, and they will either throw away their lances to take to the sabre, and then be on equal terms, or try to keep their lances and be at a great disadvantage'. He cited two occasions when his own lancers had encountered Russian and Prussian lancers on a road bordered with ditches; he engaged them with carbine-fire and then with the sabre rather than use his own lances, and, once in amongst the enemy in a relatively confined space, his troopers cut them down with hardly any danger to themselves.

A further disadvantage of the lance was that it could be lost when it penetrated an enemy's body. The first lances issued to Napoleon's Guard had a flattened 'ball' below the point that might have prevented over-penetration, but this did not feature in the 1812-pattern lance. De Brack recalled how one of his men, at Reichenbach in May 1813, refused to let his lance go after running through an enemy, and in his attempts to disengage it he was carried into the opposing ranks and killed. (On another occasion, near Lille, one of his men did let the lance go, and subsequently was only able to retrieve it by pushing it right through his enemy's body ...)

MAMELUKES & COSSACKS

Mamelukes

Two varieties of light cavalry involved in the Napoleonic Wars were unlike the general type, and involved particular tactical abilities. One of the most distinctive, albeit prominent in only one theatre of war, was the Mamelukes encountered by Napoleon's expedition to Egypt (1798–1801). Recruited from Caucasians, these warriors had been resident in Egypt from the 13th century; originally intended as a military elite in the service of the reigning sultan, they usurped his power and took over the land, retaining much of their authority even after the Turkish conquest of 1517. Replenished by a constant supply of boys from the Caucasus, they formed a warrior caste that dominated the native inhabitants and produced a force of around 10,000 light cavalry.

Equipped in an almost medieval fashion, sometimes including a mail coat and iron helmet, the individual Mameluke was an expert horseman and swordsman and a most formidable opponent. Armed with curved sabres of high quality, they could out-fence most conventional cavalry, and some remarkable feats were recorded – at the battle of the Pyramids in July 1798 one *kyacheff* (provincial governor or senior commander) was said to have actually sliced through muskets. Their armament also included carbines (often of bell-mouth design), pistols, and light javelins (a weapon sometimes styled a '*jereed*'), and each Mameluke was accompanied by two or more dismounted servants or *serradj*.

A Mameluke fires one of his several pistols in the middle of a cavalry mêlée. (Print after Horace Vernet)

Though individually so formidable, the Mameluke had no more sophisticated tactic than a headlong charge of almost suicidal bravery, firing his carbine and several pairs of pistols, then throwing his javelins before closing with the sabre; the *serradj* followed to retrieve their masters' firearms, dropped after discharge, and to dispatch any surviving enemy. Heroism and skill-at-arms could not overcome disciplined formations, however, and when sent against Napoleon's infantry formed in square the Mameluke charges foundered at terrible cost. Their reputation as warriors survived, and some who accompanied Napoleon's army back to France were incorporated into the Imperial Guard alongside the Chasseurs à Cheval. This small Mameluke element was retained throughout Napolon's reign (see Men-at-Arms 429, *Napoleon's Mamelukes*); they continued to use traditional costume and weapons, and provided perhaps the most exotically colourful unit in his army. Latterly, however, it was impossible to replace losses among the 'genuine' Mamelukes (Caucasians, North Africans and Levantines), so Frenchmen were admitted to their ranks.

The principal, indeed the only Mameluke tactic – an all-out charge. Although intensely heroic, such tactics foundered on the disciplined squares of French infantry that they encountered during Napoleon's Egyptian expedition. (Print after Joseph Beuzon)

A classic depiction of a Cossack, with his characteristically small but hardy pony; note the padded saddle. In addition to his lance he carries a pistol at his belt, and what may be a British 1796-pattern light cavalry sabre – quantities of these were sent to Russia. (Print after Horace Vernet)

COSSACKS

One of the most distinctive types of light cavalry formed an invaluable resource unique to the Russian army: the Cossacks. Light-horse service was a hereditary skill among the regional communities that provided their military force, the largest 'host' being the Cossacks of the Don, with other settlements ranging from the Ukraine in the west to the Siberian Cossacks from east of the Ural Mountains.

Many commentators at the time criticized their lack of discipline and insatiable plundering, but their military value was undoubted. Sir Robert Wilson, who served alongside them, presented the alternative view of the Cossack:

> His military virtues are splendid in common with the Russian nation; but hereditary habits of war, and perhaps a natural talent for that species of it in which they are generally engaged, adds an acute intelligence and capacity that is not generally shared. By the stars, the wind, and an [sic] union of the most ingenious observations, he travels over countries unknown to him, through forests almost impervious, and reaches his destination, or tracks some precursor that he is directed to pursue with the assurance and indefatigable ardour of the instinctive blood-hound. Nothing can elude his activity, escape his penetration, or surprise his vigilance... Mounted on a very little, ill-conditioned, but well-bred horse, which can [either] walk at the rate of five miles an hour with ease, or, in his speed, dispute the race with the swiftest – with a short whip on his wrist (as he wears no spur) – armed with a lance, a pistol in his girdle, and a sword, he never fears a competitor in single combat; but in the late war he irresistably attacked every opposing squadron in the field. Terror preceded his charge, and in vain discipline endeavoured to present an impediment to the protruding pikes. [19]

A typical contemporary view of Cossacks reconnoitering. In reconnaissance few light cavalry in Europe were their equal, and in general Russian commanders harnessed the natural skills that more than compensated for their lack of conventional cavalry training. For outpost work they sometimes operated alongside Russian light infantry, and there were occasions when riders each took an infantryman up behind the saddle to speed up a move across country.

Wilson said of their skill-at-arms that 'the Cossaque [sic] is not first armed with a lance when he proceeds to war, or when he attains manhood: it is the toy of his infancy, and the constant exercise of his youth; so that he wields it, although from 14 to 18 feet in length, with the address and freedom that the best swordsman in Europe would use his weapon ... under the guidance of an [sic] horseman so powerful and dexterous [the lance] becomes invincible but by fire, and the presuming enemy, who rashly adventures an unequal contest, will perish or obtain an inglorious experience'.

Marmont concurred, remarking that Cossack skills were inherent; they were 'a light, admirable, indefatigable and intelligent cavalry; they know how to direct their course with precision, how to scour the country, to observe everything that passes, and provide for themselves. They cannot be compared with any light troops systematically trained, they are formed by nature, and their intelligence is developed by their daily wants'.

In consequence, Cossacks did not undergo the training nor exhibit the discipline of ordinary light cavalry, as Wilson observed:

But although [they], on some occasions, have discomfited, by direct attacks, regular cavalry, it must not be supposed that they are calculated to act generally in line. Their service is of a different character, which requires a greater latitude and liberty of operation. They act in dispersion, and when they do re-unite to charge, it is not with a systematic formation, but *en masse*, or what in Germany is called the swarm attack; but even then the order should originate from their own officers, who best know their genius and powers, or, which is frequently the case, be the effect of a voluntary impulse that simultaneously animates the whole body, and which is expressed by a yell of excitement more frightful and terrific than the war-hoop [sic] of the Canadian savage.

Here Wilson touches on an important aspect of the Cossacks' value: their reputation, warranted or not. They were regarded by many as unduly savage, and thus their appearance alone, or the Cossack war-cry of '*Hurrah!*', could throw their opponents into confusion. It was the threat of a Cossack attack that paralysed Napoleon's extreme left wing at Borodino; although it was initially thought to have achieved little, the wide flanking movement of the Cossack Hetman Platov and Gen Uvarov had a marked effect on Napoleon's conduct of the battle by its mere presence.

Attempts were made to introduce more conventional aspects into the Cossack forces (Wilson highlighted in particular the introduction of uniform distinctions for the various Cossack corps). However, Marmont was among those who thought that such attempts tended to cramp their inherent skills – a factor also believed to affect the abilities of other 'irregular' troops upon whom more conventional forms of training and discipline were imposed. Marmont also believed that the fact that Russia possessed such a huge, unique and expert resource tended to reduce the capabilities of their conventional light cavalry: as they alone were not relied upon to conduct reconnaissance and skirmishing duties, there was a tendency for them to become more 'line' cavalry than specifically 'light'. (The Cossacks of the Guard were, in fact, conventionally trained and uniformly clothed and equipped, unlike most of the other corps.)

A common tactic was to deploy Cossack units as a screen in advance of conventional forces, like ordinary skirmishers, and to use them to secure an army's flanks. In combat, Suvarov recommended that they were held at the rear of the conventional cavalry as a third line, or on the flanks, to assail the enemy's flanks during the initial action and to pursue once the enemy had given way. When acting as a primary force rather than as a support, Cossack units might form in a single rank calculated to exceed the frontage of the enemy, so that when collision occurred they could exert extra pressure by lapping around the enemy's flanks. It was remarked that in the advance they might follow a curving path rather than a straight course, so that the enemy might be deceived as to their principal intention.

Because the Cossacks were not generally trained in the most conventional of cavalry tactics, and from the nature of their small mounts, contemporary wisdom held that they would rarely engage resolute, formed troops. A typical example of this belief was recounted by Denis Davydov, one of the most noted leaders of Russian light horse, who described an occasion when his command, principally Cossacks, attempted to engage Napoleon's Guard cavalry, which maintained their close columns as the Russians hovered. Numbers of Russian officers and ordinary Cossacks rode at them, but were driven off with carbine-fire; Davydov stated that the French just laughed at the Cossack style of combat and ploughed on unhindered, like a ship-of-the-line amongst fishing boats.

There were occasions when Cossacks did engage formed troops while retaining elements of their particular tactics, and an example was recorded by Eugène Labaume, three days before Borodino. Observing Russian forces in a wood, 'the Viceroy [Gen Eugène de Beauharnais, commanding IV Corps] ordered Col Rambourgh, of the 3rd Italian Chasseurs, to march towards it, and bring them to action. The Cossacks observed this movement without being intimidated, and when the chasseurs were on the point of coming up with them, they rushed from the wood, crying "*Houra! houra!*" – a cry become famous, and which these barbarians always use when they charge their enemies. The Italian chasseurs received them with great coolness. The action was smart, but of no duration, for the Cossacks seeing the Bavarian light-horse advance, quitted the field, leaving in our possession a few prisoners'.[20]

Skirmishing on the battlefield aside, a principal service of the Cossacks was in reconnaissance and raids, in which their hit-and-run tactics could be devastating. One of the best examples of the latter was the unrelenting harassment of the retiring Grande Armée in 1812, when flying columns of Cossacks and hussars drove Napoleon's army to destruction. A perpetual terror, they cut off stragglers and gave the retreating forces no respite, their threat heightened by the

Cossacks with a local guide during the 1813 campaign in Germany. Their costumes and weapons are characteristic, including the lance, pistols, sabre, and in one case a slung carbine; the foreground rider carries the Cossack *nagaika* whip, used instead of spurs. Note his high 'seat' due to the pad-saddle. (Print after J.A. Klein)

trepidation caused by even the chance of Cossack attack. Early in the French retreat from Moscow, on 25 October, a force of Cossacks surprised the Emperor while he was reconnoitering, and although he was saved by his escort it was one of the closest escapes he ever had.

Although most effective when mounted, Cossacks could also be employed as dismounted skirmishers. One commentator praised their ability to dismount, shoot and remount: 'the men were on and off their horses with an agility, dexterity, and rapidity, which baffles all description'. It was stated that on one occasion Suvarov ordered his Cossacks to cut their lances in half to use them as pikes for dismounted service, stating that if they were killed they would have no need of lances and, if victorious, they could easily obtain more.

Associated with the Cossacks, but much less effective, were the large numbers of Asiatic tribesmen employed in the Russian army and generally known as Bashkirs. Their principal weapon was the bow, which led the French to bestow on them the nicknames 'les Amours' or 'Cupidons du Nord' ('northern Cupids'). Marbot expressed a common opinion:

In a moment the barbarians surrounded our squadrons with loud shouts, letting off thousands of arrows ... the Bashkirs are totally undrilled and have no more notion of any formation than a flock of sheep. Thus they cannot shoot horizontally in front of them without hitting their own comrades, and are obliged to fire their arrows parabolically into the air [so that] nine-tenths of the arrows are lost, while the few that hit are pretty well spent ... so that the wounds they cause are usually trifling [Marbot himself was slightly wounded by a Bashkir arrow]. As they have no other weapons, they are certainly the least dangerous troops in the world. However, as they were coming up in myriads, and the more of these wasps one killed the more came on, the vast number of arrows with which they filled the air were bound sooner or later to inflict some severe wounds.[21]

LIGHT CAVALRY TASKS

RECONNAISSANCE

Reconnaissance was one of the primary functions of light cavalry, whose fast-moving units preceded the advance of an army and covered its flanks. The forces involved could range from small patrols to entire regiments, and it was for such duties that light cavalry were deployed as corps cavalry or as part of heavy-cavalry formations that were themselves less able to perform such tasks. Typical reconnaissance practice was described in the British cavalry regulations:

The conduct of an advanced guard of an officer and 40 or 50 men, may show the general principles on which more considerable bodies are to act on the same service.

Reconnoitering in cold weather, French 5e Hussards wearing the pelisse as a jacket. Note the pair of advance scouts riding ahead of the main detachment. (Print after Edouard Detaille)

The advanced guard in general marches about two hundred yards in front of the column, regiment, or smaller body; but the distance must depend upon the nature of the country, which when woody, makes it necessary to remain nearer the main body, than when it is free from enclosures.

From the advanced guard, the officer detaches to his front, a serjeant and twelve men, who are to preserve the same distance from the officer's party, that the officer is from the column. The serjeant is in like manner to send two men forward, and detach two others, one at each flank, as side patroles [sic], who are to keep in a line with those men most in advance. The officer will, for the same purpose, detach one non-commissioned officer and four men, on each of his flanks. The side patroles are distant between three and four hundred yards on the flanks, which distance varies according to the places they have to examine, and the impediments met with on the march. They are not to lose sight of each other for any length of time, but to take advantage of every height to look round them, and see that they preserve a corresponding line with each other, and the march of the advance guard. The patroles must examine all villages, hollow ways and woods, that lie in the direction of their march; taking care to reconnoitre from the heights, the country below, before they descend into the vallies [sic]. As soon as the enemy is perceived, the person who discovers him, must fire a pistol to announce it; when the non-commission [sic] officer of the party will ride to the spot, and having made his observations, send a correct report of what he has seen to the officer, who is to convey it to the officer commanding the column.

It is a necessary precaution to send out side patroles from the column, and likewise a rear guard, when it is possible for an enemy to approach in that direction. The rear guard is to be conducted on the same principles directed for the advance.

Such basic principles were observed universally, even when the numbers and distances involved were much greater.

Austrian trooper of the 2nd Hussars 'Erzherzog Joseph' prepared for skirmishing, with his short carbine on his hip and his drawn sabre hanging from his wrist. (Print after R. von Ottenfeld)

As well as carrying out reconnaissance missions themselves, light cavalrymen were often provided as escorts for officers who rode out to reconnoitre. In this winter scene hussars hold the horses of two officers who have gone forward on foot to use telescopes from a vantage-point. (Print after Meissonier)

Again with staff officers reconnoitering in the background, this depicts a Prussian hussar (right) in the brown pelisse of Hussar Regt No. 4 (1st Silesian) greeting a dragoon wearing a light blue *Litewka*. In the Russian campaign the Prussian contingent serving in Napoleon's X Corps included the 3rd Combined Hussars, formed from squadrons of Regts Nos. 4 & 6 (1st & 2nd Silesian). (Print after Rozat de Mandres)

OUTPOSTS

Similar care was required in so-called 'outpost' duty, a more static form of reconnaissance in which a screen of light cavalry would both conceal the dispositions of an encampment from the enemy, and give notice of, and blunt the first thrust of, any enemy raid. Such service demanded both skill and experience, which were not always available. For example, William Tomkinson recalled that 'to attempt giving men or officers any idea in England in outpost duty was considered absurd, and when they came abroad, they all had this to learn. The fact was, there was no one to teach them. Sir Stapleton Cotton, at Woodbridge in Suffolk, with the 14th and 16th Light Dragoons, tried and got the enemy's vedettes and his own looking the same way'.[22] Another perhaps not uncommon factor was quoted by Charles Palmer of the British 10th Hussars, who in the Peninsula sent out a reconnaissance party 'to learn the state of affairs in a pretty large town near the army; they remained so long without returning, that he dispatched another party [which] found them all beastly drunk, and their horses tied up in different parts of the town in the most disgraceful situation'.[23]

Leadership was also quoted as an important factor, and the fact that some officers were noted for their particular expertise suggests that 'outpost' skills might not be exploited to the full under more lax commanders. For example, Gen Auguste de Colbert was cited as possessing especial skills in this regard; he led Ney's advance guard with such courage and distinction in the Jena campaign that the marshal remarked that he always slept peacefully when Colbert was in command of his outposts. Conversely, Gen Horace François Sébastiani was said to be so careless in the supervision of his outposts – leading to the enemy's rough handling of his troops at Vinkovo, for example – that he was ironically nicknamed 'General Surprise' (meaning 'Surprised').

The ideal 'outpost' commander would seem to have been like the officer of the 1st Hussars of the King's German Legion, a regiment acknowledged as unmatched in its field, who was quoted by John Kincaid. In an exchange during the Peninsular War the German officer asked Sydney Beckwith of the British 95th Rifles how he was. 'Tolerably well, thank you, considering that I am obliged to sleep with one eye open'. 'By ----', replied the hussar, 'I never sleeps [sic] at all!' A story was told of the same officer that exemplifies the best practice of an outpost commander: when he was seen to be preparing to sleep fully dressed even after the end of hostilities, a staff officer remarked, 'Surely you don't mean to sleep in your clothes tonight, when you know there is an armistice?' 'Air mistress or no air mistress', replied the German, 'I sleeps [sic] in my breeches!'

So expert were these German professional light cavalry in comparison with some of their British colleagues that in describing them Kincaid summarized the attributes of the ideal light horsemen, irrespective of nationality: 'I would rather have dispensed with my dinner (however sharp set) than the services of one of those thoroughbred soldiers, for they were as singularly intelligent and useful on outpost duty, as they were effective and daring in the field'.[24]

VEDETTES

De Brack commented on what might be styled 'best practice' in the posting of vedettes (cavalry outposts or sentries). A 'small post' of a corporal and three or four men, or even individual sentries, should be posted some distance from the main post or 'grand guard' of the unit that provided the reconnaissance force, which would be ready at a moment's notice to support the small posts if they were attacked. Signals in the first instance should be made by firing a shot, or, to convey more complex intelligence, a rider should be sent to the grand guard. Especial vigilance was required at daybreak and twilight, when attacks could be mounted almost unseen, and commanders of posts should ensure that their information was accurate, lest they fall into the traps of either overlooking a genuine attack, or rousing the entire army on a false alarm.

Reconnaissance, claimed de Brack, was not just a matter of seeing, but seeing correctly. It was often more effective to use two scouts than 200, so that they might not be spotted by the enemy. Individual vedettes should observe from under cover, and remove their lance-pennon lest it reveal their position to the enemy. Single vedettes should be relieved every hour, and a four-man 'small post' every four hours (so that each man had only a

1815: a local peasant brought in by a trooper of the French 3e Hussards is questioned by an officer in the detachment's bivouac – a temporary camp of the type suitable for a light cavalry outpost. In a period when road signposting was minimal and maps were neither widely available nor generally accurate, reconnaissance detachments often had to rely on local guides. Note the tall, cylindrical *shako rouleau*; although never a regulation item, this became increasingly popular from 1812 onwards. (Print after Vernet)

Skirmishers of the French 4e Hussards. When firing the carbine from the saddle it was important to keep ones mount facing the enemy so as to present a smaller target. Some authorities recommended that the carbine be fired to the right of the horse's head so as to avoid sparks from the priming burning it and making it start; others recommended firing to the left front, which was easier from a right-shouldered pose. (Print after Hippolyte Bellangé)

one-hour spell of extreme concentration). During the hours of darkness the distance between army, grand guard, small posts and individual vedettes should be reduced. Two-man patrols should march in silence and single file, carbine in hand so that it did not rattle against other equipment; they were to preserve complete silence so as not to alert the enemy, including the avoidance of metalled road-surfaces. De Brack said that in the Peninsula, where the ground was rocky, patrols would deaden the sound of their horses' footfall by wrapping sheepskin around their hooves.

The transmission of intelligence from advanced vedettes to their supporting body might not always rely upon shots or the physical passing of messages. Visible manoeuvres by vedettes, such as circling in a particular direction, might have an agreed meaning to the watchers, and movements of a lance could be used to transmit basic signals. (A slightly different and particularly audacious use of the weapon was recorded at Quatre Bras, where the position of British infantry was hidden by a tall crop of rye. To mark their position so that French cavalry could regulate the various stages of their charge to hit them with maximum impetus, at least one lancer rode almost onto the bayonets, and stuck a lance upright in the ground to mark the redcoats' position for the following troopers.)

Patrol clashes

The light cavalry's role in reconnaissance and patrolling along the front and flanks of an army could lead to an almost endless succession of low-level skirmishing with troops performing the same duty for the enemy. Such engagements, often involving only small numbers but significant in a minor way, were often unrecorded and unremarked. As an example, the following is taken from Austrian dispatches from the Netherlands in late August 1793:

> A very strong patrole [sic] of the enemy, consisting of both cavalry and infantry, having at four o'clock on the morning of the 26th, fallen in with a weak patrole of our chasseurs near Templeuve, the cavalry at first attacked the chasseurs and took some of them prisoners; but Captain Bechtold having speedily advanced at the head of a detachment of the cuirassiers of Cavanagh, he took the enemy's patrole in flank, notwithstanding their continued fire, and put the French cavalry to flight. Captain Bechtold, with 30 cuirassiers, then fell upon the infantry, 40 of whom he killed on the spot, and took one officer and 40 men prisoners, and dispersed the rest. On our side there were eight chasseurs killed or missing, and two chasseurs and two carabiniers wounded.
>
> One of our patroles, consisting of 20 hussars of the regiment of the Emperor, and the light horse of Lobtowitz, with 22 men of the regiment of Kaunitz, having, in Capel, fallen in with a patrole of the enemy, consisting of 30 cavalry and 40 infantry, our cavalry attacked them with so much bravery, that they cut to pieces 20 men, and took nine prisoners, besides one officer of cavalry. The rest fled towards Pont-a-Marque.[25]

Such minor engagements involving cavalry patrols and vedettes, and light infantry picquets, were a universal feature of campaigning throughout the period, and represented an important part of light cavalry service.

SKIRMISHING

Although all but the heaviest cavalry could perform skirmishing duty, it was one of the most important aspects of light cavalry service, and involved the use of both carbines and pistols. Most carbines had very limited range due to the short barrels used in order to facilitate their handling on horseback, and carbines might even be fired one-handed so that the left hand could hold the reins (even if the carbine barrel was supported on the

Austrian hussar skirmisher, 1813/14. His carbine is hooked to the crossbelt by the spring clip, and outside his hip its ramrod hangs from the belt by a narrow white strap. The sabre bounces around distractingly from its sword-knot looped around his wrist; the French commentator Fortuné de Brack thought it better to tie the sabre to the wrist with a long, twisted handkerchief, which would better absorb a sabre-cut. (Print after R. von Ottenfeld)

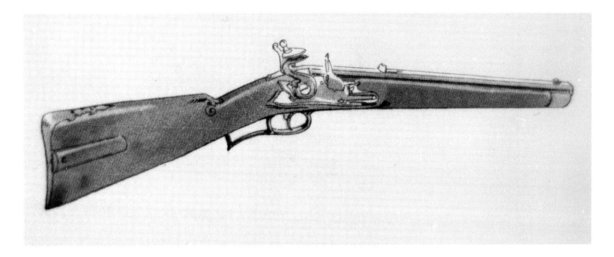

The Austrian 1789 model *Cavallerie-Stutzen*, a very short rifled carbine issued to a small number of men in each squadron. This, and the 1798 pattern that succeeded it, measured only 69cm (27in) overall, compared with the 85.2cm-long (33.5in) 1798 smoothbore hussar carbine. (Print after R. von Ottenfeld)

left forearm). Carbines were thus inaccurate even when compared to the infantry musket of the day, and especially when fired from horseback; a British regulation noted that cavalry skirmish-fire was 'more a demonstration than an effectual mode of offence'. As one writer commented, 'a man who is a tolerably fair shot on his own legs, may find himself as much puzzled upon a shy or hot-tempered horse, as a horse-artillery-man would be perplexed to take a good aim with an 18-pounder in a heavy sea on board of ship'.[26]

The practice of keeping the sword drawn and suspended from the wrist during skirmishing served to further impede the use of a firearm (and as de Brack noted, might accidentally wound either horse or rider). It was also remarked that when men were skirmishing with pistols they often lost them, through having to drop them in order to catch up the sabre in an emergency. It was noted that Cossacks avoided this accidental loss by attaching their pistols to a cord over the shoulder. In consequence, skirmish-fire was often as ineffective as that described by Cavalié Mercer during the retreat from Quatre Bras:

G **BRITISH HUSSAR REGIMENT SKIRMISHING**

Although there were different modes of selecting and deploying skirmishers in the various armies, skirmishing practice was similar throughout. This schematic depicts such common practice, in this case applied by a British hussar unit of four squadrons, according to the detailed instructions specified by the cavalry regulations.

(1) The regiment is arrayed in line, with skirmishers drawn from each of the four squadrons. Sufficient gaps are left between squadrons to permit the skirmishers to fall back without disordering the main body, and then either to rejoin their particular squadrons or to assemble as a body in the rear.

(2) When skirmishers were sent out, they rode forward to positions about 150 yards in front of the main body of their squadron. A number of them then advanced about 100 yards further, the remainder standing fast to provide a reserve for the skirmish line.

(3) The skirmishers then extended to link up and cover the whole of the regiment's frontage, and formed two ranks about 50 yards apart, with wide gaps between the files. When the enemy was in range, the front rank fired only when the

rear rank was loaded, the front rank being informed of this by the verbal command 'Ready'. In advancing, the rear rank passed through the gaps in the front rank, rode some 50 yards ahead, and themselves fired; these movements were controlled by officers and sergeants posted between the two ranks of skirmishers, who signalled the advance of the rear rank by a verbal command and 'a wide signal with [the] sword'. The same applied in reverse when skirmishers were withdrawing, as when covering a retreat.

(Inset 1) A trooper of the 15th Hussars, *c.*1812, reloading his carbine in the saddle; they were ordered not to try to accomplish this while on the move, but were otherwise supposed to keep moving so as not to present a static target.

(Inset 2) This depicts the dismounted use of one of the few effective firearms used by light cavalry: the Baker rifled carbine, as carried by some British hussar regiments including the 10th (illustrated). During the retreat from Quatre Bras on 17 June 1815 this regiment dismounted its skirmishers to block the bridge over the river Thy, discouraging the French pursuit with rifle-fire.

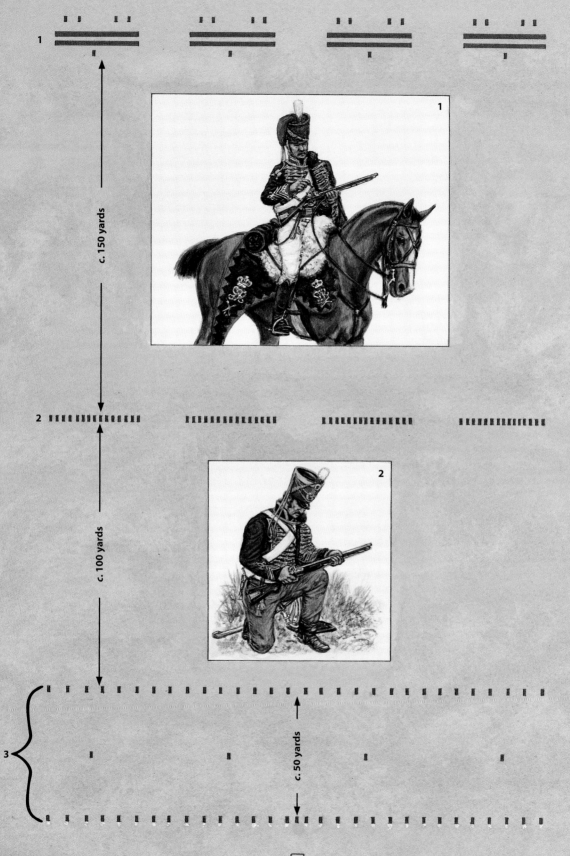

1

c. 150 yards

1

2

c. 100 yards

2

3

c. 50 yards

Two double lines of skirmishers extended all along the bottom [of a shallow valley] – the foremost of each line were within a few yards of each other – constantly in motion, riding backwards and forwards, firing their carbines and pistols, and then reloading, still on the move. This fire seemed to me to be more dangerous for those on the hills above than for us below; for all, both French and English, generally stuck out their carbines or pistols as they continued to move backwards and forwards, and discharged them without taking any particular aim, and mostly in the air. I did not see a man fall on either side; the thing appeared quite ridiculous; and but for hearing the bullets whizzing overhead, one might have fancied it no more than a sham-fight.[27]

This underlines the fact that the main purpose of skirmishing was not to inflict casualties, but merely to establish a forward position to deter enemy encroachment, and to screen or conceal the position of the main body.

A typical deployment for skirmishing on horseback is described and illustrated as Plate G. As a general principle, skirmishers were usually deployed in two ranks, with wide gaps between files, so that one rank was always loaded while the other was reloading. In advancing or retreating, one rank passed through the gaps in the other, which covered it during the movement. Even when holding the same position throughout, the formation was constantly in motion, as the 'loaded' rank moved forwards and the other fell back to reload.

De Brack noted that although this process was practised on the drill-ground, in one aspect it was both impractical and dangerous in action: when retreating, the first to retire should be those mounted on the weakest horses, so that the best-mounted men would always form the rearguard, providing that this variation from the established drill could be accomplished without causing the withdrawal to be uneven. He observed that it was a general practice for skirmishers to close up when retreating, whereas the Cossacks closed up to charge but dispersed when retiring. This was more effective, because skirmishers who bunched up as they retired often fell over each other in their haste, and were unable to use their weapons freely if packed together, and so were unduly vulnerable to the pursuing enemy. By implication, this suggested that only when out of immediate danger should retreating skirmishers be called to rally.

Dismounted fire

Cavalry firearms were probably most effective when the men were dismounted and acted as light infantry, though this process would usually involve at least one-third of the strength being kept out of the fight to hold the horses of the dismounted men. The ability of the French light cavalry in particular to fight on foot was remarked on by a number of their opponents; for example, during the 1814 campaign in France 'many Austrian officers ...

French trooper of the 4e Hussards skirmishing with the pistol. Note that he holds the weapon with its right side uppermost, which might help the transmission of priming powder from the pan through the touch-hole and into the barrel. (Print by Martinet)

British light dragoons skirmishing, *c.* 1798. Note that the front rank are discharging their pistols, while the corporal at the rear (his rank indicated at this date by two straight stripes across his upper sleeve) readies his carbine. (Engraving by Sadler after Thomas Rowlandson)

can attest how severely on several occasions they smarted from it, when, linking bridles, [the French] performed the duties of light infantry. If worsted, they galloped off; whereas, if the heavy column on which they were practicing as a target threw out its skirmishers to repel them, down they were, sabring away, in a twinkling'.[28]

Opinions on the cavalry's use of firearms were mixed. Marmont, for example, stated that they were almost superfluous and only of use as a means of signalling. Conversely, a writer in the *British Military Library or Journal* described a combination of mounted and dismounted tactics against infantry in square:

> A part of them dismount to attack a flank or face of the square formed by the infantry. These dismounted horsemen take a position parallel to the flank or face, at the distance of 250 paces, with intervals of twelve paces between the different platoons, composed of twenty files, and begin to advance under alternate firing, while the rest on horseback observe the square at a distance of 300 paces. As the dismounted horsemen may be superior in number to one of the flanks or faces of the square; as they moreover concentrate their fire against the square, without being from their intervals much exposed to that of the infantry, the foot who form the flank or face attacked, will probably fall into confusion, and afford the mounted cavalry, which advances through the intervals of the dismounted horsemen, a favourable opportunity of making a successful attack.[29]

Firing from the saddle

As discussed under Plate H, there were occasions when cavalry employed fire when attempting to blunt an enemy advance. Some were critical of this tactic: Warnery stated that cavalry musketry was fit only to frighten sparrows, and that it required only a few horses to be frightened by the noise for a whole squadron to be thrown into disorder. There was also a suggestion that this tactic was a sign of irresolution, by contrast to a forward movement

A French *général de brigade* with a hussar orderly, the latter providing a good view of the carriage of the 1786 pattern carbine. The light-cavalry *mousqueton* was suspended from the outer of the paired shoulderbelts by means of a spring clip engaging with a ring sliding along a rail screwed to the left side of the stock. Note the small additional securing strap around the small of the stock, and also the cartridge pouch left of the butt, suspended from the inner shoulderbelt. The carbine is carried loaded and primed, with the pan closed and the hammer in half-cock position. The 1786 pattern had a barrel length of 70cm (27.4in), potentially giving it a longer accurate range than the 16in barrel of the British Paget. (Print by Martinet)

immediately to engage blade-to-blade. French cavalry that attempted this perhaps demonstrated the point in an action in the Peninsula in May 1809, when two squadrons of the British 16th Light Dragoons confronted four French squadrons covering a withdrawal (two in advance and the remainder in support), as described by William Tomkinson:

The instant we saw the enemy from the top of the hill, the word was given. The men set up an huzzah, and advanced to the charge. The enemy fired a volley at us when [we were] about fifty yards from them, and then went about, setting off as hard as they could ride, we pursuing, cutting at them, and making all the prisoners in our power. The other two squadrons in support went about, and the whole retired in no small confusion. The affair was more like a skirmish at a field day than an affair with the enemy. From the enemy being in such haste with their fire, all the shots went over our heads.[30]

H VOLLEY-FIRING FROM THE SADDLE

A common adage of the period held that cavalry should never receive a charge at the halt lest they be swept away by the impetus of the enemy, but should always meet an attack on the move. Nevertheless, there were occasions on which an approaching enemy was met from the halt by carbine-fire. One of the best-known accounts of such incidents is that by Charles Parquin of the 20e Chasseurs à Cheval, which met an oncoming Russian charge with a volley at Eylau in February 1807. The circumstances that day particularly favoured such a tactic: the approaching enemy was moving at no more than a walk due to the snow and soft ground, thus greatly reducing their impetus and giving the defending French more time. Clearly, firing in this way was not an end in itself, but if the carbine-fire did not actually stop the enemy it might at least disorder them. This would make them vulnerable to a countercharge by the defenders, launched as soon as the volley had been fired, so that the disrupted incoming charge could be met on the move as conventional wisdom suggested.

By contrast, the danger of awaiting a charge at the halt is exemplified by the action at Sahagun in December 1808, when eight French squadrons – 1er Régiment Provisional de Chasseurs à Cheval in the first line, 8e Dragons behind them – engaged the advancing British 15th Hussars with their carbines. This fire seems to have had little effect, since the 15th's charge routed them: 'The shock was terrible; horses and men were overthrown, and a shriek of terror, intermixed with oaths, groans, and prayers for mercy, issued from the whole extent of their front.'[31]

(Inset) Depicting the French 5e Chasseurs à Cheval in 1806, this shows the use of the carbine (*mousqueton*) when mounted. It was customary to keep the weapon attached to the outer shoulder belt by means of the spring clip, ring and rail, so that the carbine would not be lost if the trooper had to drop it to use his sabre. Both this practice, and that of keeping the sabre looped to the wrist, must have hampered aiming and reloading. The uniform shown includes a braided dolman, used at times by French Chasseurs à Cheval in imitation of hussar style.

c. 100 metres

PURSUIT

It was after the enemy had broken that another of the light cavalry's particular attributes came into play: the ability to pursue rapidly, and to complete a rout. This was important, since, as Marmont stated, 'an enemy in flight can always rally, if they cannot be readily come up to at the moment of disorder'. Light cavalry were ideal for pursuit, both on the battlefield and beyond it.

In the period immediately after the dispersal of an enemy force the need for good order was paramount, so that a protracted pursuit could be performed in formation and with less risk from counterattack. This was sometimes difficult, as described by Alexander Gordon of the British 15th Hussars' pursuit of broken French cavalry at Sahagun: 'Having rode together nearly a mile, pell-mell, cutting and slashing at each other, it appeared to me indispensable that order should be re-established, as the men were quite wild and the horses almost blown; therefore ... I pressed through the throng until I overtook and halted those who were the farthest advanced in pursuit. As soon as I had accomplished this object, the bugles sounded the "rally"' – but when Gordon looked around he could not see a single formed body on the field, and it was fortunate that there was no French reserve to sweep away the scattered hussars.[32]

The concept of pursuit after victory could be applied in a much more profound manner than a chase of a few miles off a battlefield. Light cavalry, who were able to move quickly and had no need for much support, were the key to such a strategic pursuit. The most notable of such operations was probably the French pursuit and destruction of the Prussian forces following their defeat at Jena-Auerstädt in October 1806, in which the light cavalry played a vital role (though other arms were also involved). Admittedly, much of the Prussian army and its commanders were demoralized, but it is still remarkable that in three weeks of manoeuvre, rapid marches and relatively minor engagements the French took some 140,000 prisoners. One of the most audacious episodes involved the light cavalry brigade (5e and 7e Hussards) of Gen Antoine Lasalle, part of Murat's Reserve Cavalry. Lasalle raced ahead to the fortress of Stettin, whose defenders greatly outnumbered his two regiments, and demanded its surrender. Despite the strength of the position its governor fell for the bluff and capitulated, leading Napoleon to comment to Murat that if his light cavalry could take fortresses, he might as well disband his engineers and melt down his heavy guns.

Infantry caught out of square or solid column formation (as was often the case during the pursuit of a beaten force) was terribly vulnerable. This artist's impression shows the loss of the 'Eagle' of the French 55e de Ligne at Heilsberg in June 1807, to the Prussian Hussar Regt No. 5 'Prittwitz'. These 'black hussars' with their death's-head insignia were also nicknamed *'Der ganze Todt'* – 'the complete death'. (Print after Richard Knötel)

TACTICS IN PRACTICE

It is possible to identify relatively minor actions in which all aspects of versatile light cavalry service were required, from reconnaissance to skirmishing both mounted and on foot, charges, flank attacks, rallies and pursuits, involving the necessity of maintaining order, independent action by sub-units, and the initiative demanded of junior commanders. All these factors are evident in some relatively little-known episodes during the closing stages of the Peninsular War, about which a number of valuable eyewitness accounts appeared in the *United Service Journal* for 1840–41, written in relation to William Napier's version of the events in question.

St Martyn de la Touch, 28 March 1814

As Wellington was advancing upon Toulouse, Marshal Soult employed a screen of light cavalry and infantry to deny him crossings over the rivers that protected that city, including the Garonne, Ariège, Giron, Touch and Ers. The troops involved in the resulting actions were not elite units but ordinary light cavalry – indeed, the British 18th Hussars were relatively new to the war, and their recent performance had been roundly castigated by Wellington.

On 28 March, to screen the movements of his infantry, Wellington ordered the light cavalry brigade of Sir Richard Hussey Vivian to watch the French light horse holding the bridge at St Martyn de la Touch. When Vivian noticed the withdrawal of French vedettes he presumed that they had discovered the movements of Wellington's army, so he determined to distract them by seizing the river crossing. To this end he advanced with the 18th Hussars, while sending two squadrons of the 1st King's German Legion Hussars to attempt to ford the river below the village and take the enemy in the flank.

Once through the village, Vivian discovered that the bridge was barricaded, with French skirmishers beyond it firing upon him from rising ground that overlooked him. He ordered part of the 18th to dismount and skirmish on foot – some to engage the enemy skirmishers, and another party to rush the bridge. Led by Lt Lionel Dawson, the latter detachment took the bridge and dismantled the barricade, and were so enthused by their 'light infantry' service that they began to ascend the hill towards the French sharpshooters. Vivian followed them and ordered them to retire and remount; then he pushed on with a

Trooper of the British 15th Hussars priming the pan of his carbine while skirmishing on horseback, as the 18th Hussars did during their advance on the 22e Chasseurs à Cheval holding the near bank of the Ers river on 8 April 1814. (Engraving by Stadler after Charles Hamilton Smith)

squadron of the 18th. At the sight of their advance a large body of French cavalry, thinking that a single squadron would only make such a move if they were supported by others, and with the German hussars approaching their flank, fired a carbine volley and then retired at a canter. Vivian pursued them for some distance, but when he came under fire from the French positions at St Cyprien, and observed a strong force of French cavalry formed by the roadside, he called off the pursuit and retired out of gunshot range. In this action the 18th Hussars suffered just one man wounded.

Croix d'Orade, 8 April 1814

This rather better-known action involved the same troops. A French light cavalry screen had been falling back gradually on both banks of the river Ers, destroying the bridges as they retired. The troops involved were the brigade of Gen Jacques Laurent Vial – 5e, 10e, 15e and 22e Chasseurs à Cheval – of which the 5e and 22e were the most closely engaged that day. Also present was Marshal Soult's cavalry commander, his brother Pierre, who possessed none of the family's military talent. The marshal would apparently blame him for what occurred on 8 April, especially as he had declined the infantry support he had been offered.

General Vivian, who had with him the same two regiments as at St Martyn de la Touch, was ordered by Wellington to push the enemy over the Ers in the vicinity of Croix d'Orade, and was told to expect infantry support. He advanced upon the river under cover of the skirmishers of the 18th Hussars, who were engaged on the near side of the river by the 22e Chasseurs. During a personal reconnaissance to gauge the enemy's strength, accompanied only by his trumpeter, Vivian strayed too close to the chasseurs and was shot in the right arm. He thought it a slight wound until he lifted his sabre, whereupon the bone fractured and he collapsed in agony; having given his orders he was carried away, leaving Maj James Hughes of the 18th Hussars in command.

Hughes continued to advance behind his skirmishers, still trying to judge the strength of the opposition. He remarked, significantly, that the main body of chasseurs met them '*as usual*, with a discharge of carbines' (author's italics), before they began to retire. Suddenly another body of chasseurs, concealed until then by the buildings of the village, came at the leading element of the 18th from their flank. To meet this threat, two half-troops of the 18th were wheeled to the left against them. The French troopers faltered; the 18th's detachments rallied, one remaining to protect the left flank while the other half-troop rejoined the main body.

Covered by the skirmishers of the 5e Chasseurs firing from the far bank, the 22e fell back upon the bridge, and momentarily they and the 18th Hussars sat their saddles facing one another. Just as British infantry came up in support, both French and British regiments sounded the charge at the same moment. The leading British squadron got into its stride first, and as the 22e Chasseurs turned away they became jammed against the bridge, losing all cohesion. Hughes described what followed as a rout, with the French suffering many casualties including more than 100 taken prisoner. As the 18th pursued them across the river the French tried to rally upon the rearmost element of their brigade, and to mount a countercharge; however, they were stopped by another squadron of the 18th which had acted as a reserve to that in the lead.

Apparently, the French counter was also impeded by a very small party from the 1st King's German Legion Hussars, an eight-man picquet led by a Sgt Westermann who had crossed a deep ditch and now menaced the

Officers of Chasseurs à Cheval, c. 1812, based on an eyewitness depiction by Christian Suhr, 'the Bourgeois of Hamburg'. The officer in the centre wears the chasseurs' plain *surtout* service coat, but the others show the hussar style that was also popular in this branch of the light cavalry. The fur *colpack* caps indicate the regiment's 1st Company, the *compagnie d'élite*. (Print after Rozat de Mandres)

chasseurs' flank. Their action demonstrates another factor of light cavalry service: because of the scattered nature of 'outpost' duty and skirmishing there were rarely enough officers to command all the small elements, so intelligent and experienced NCOs might have to act independently upon their own initiative. (Indeed, earlier in this action the half-troops of the 18th that had wheeled left to meet the threat to their flank that suddenly appeared from behind the houses seem to have been led by NCOs.)

As more of Vivian's brigade came up, and being assured that British infantry had reached the river, the 18th Hussars fell back across the bridge. As the pursuing chasseurs came up to the bridge they were met by volley-fire from redcoats crouched along the river bank; they called off the pursuit, leaving the bridge safely in British hands. Although this was a relatively minor action (the 18th lost only 3 men killed, 6 wounded and 5 missing), the seizure of the bridge at Croix d'Orade was of genuine significance, and the fight there represents in microcosm the whole spectrum of capabilities that was unique to the versatile light cavalry.

SELECT BIBLIOGRAPHY

English-language editions of foreign sources are listed.

Anon., *Instructions and Regulations for the Formations and Movements of the Cavalry* (London, 1801)

Anon., *The Light Horse Drill* (London, 1802)

Anon., *Manual for Volunteer Corps of Cavalry* (London, 1803)

Ardant du Picq, C.J.J. (trans. N. Greely & R.C. Cotton), *Battle Studies* (New York, 1921)

Bismarck, F.W. von (trans. N.L. Beamish), *Lectures on the Tactics of Cavalry* (London, 1827)

Brack, A.F. de, *Light Cavalry Outposts* (London, 1876)

Bukhari, E., *Napoleon's Dragoons and Lancers*, Men-at-Arms 55 (London, 1977)

Bukhari, E., *Napoleon's Line Chasseurs*, Men-at-Arms 68 (London, 1977)

Bukhari, E., *Napoleon's Hussars*, Men-at-Arms 76 (London, 1978)

Elting, J.R., *Swords Around a Throne: Napoleon's Grande Armée* (London, 1988)

Fletcher, I., *Galloping at Everything: The British Cavalry in the Peninsular War and at Waterloo 1808–15: A Reappraisal* (Staplehurst, 1999)

Glover, R., *Peninsular Preparation: The Reform of the British Army 1795–1809* (Cambridge, 1963)

Haythornthwaite, P.J., *British Cavalryman 1792–1815*, Warrior 8 (London, 1994)

Haythornthwaite, P.J., *Napoleonic Cavalry* (London, 2001)

Hofschroer, P., *Prussian Cavalry of the Napoleonic Wars (1) 1792–1807*, Men-at-Arms 162 (London, 1985), and *(2) 1807–15*, MAA 172 (1986)

Marbot, J.B.A.M. (trans. A.J. Butler), *The Memoirs of Baron de Marbot* (London, 1913)

Nafziger, G.F., *Imperial Bayonets: Tactics of the Napoleonic Battery, Battalion and Brigade as found in Contemporary Regulations* (London & Mechanicsburg, 1996)

Nosworthy, B., *Battle Tactics of Napoleon and his Enemies* (London, 1995)

Pawly, R., *The Red Lancers* (Ramsbury, 1998)

Rocca, A.J.M. de, *Memoirs of the War of the French in Spain* (London, 1815; r/p as *In the Peninsula with a French Hussar,* 1990)

Rogers, H.C.B., *Napoleon's Army* (London, 1974)

Rothenberg, G.E., *Napoleon's Great Adversaries: The Archduke Charles and the Austrian Army 1792 –1814* (London, 1982)

Smith, D.G., *Charge! Great Cavalry Charges of the Napoleonic Wars* (London, 2003)

Spring, L., *The Cossacks 1799–1815* (Oxford, 2003)

Warnery, K.E. von, *Remarks on Cavalry* (London, 1798; r/p with intro by B. Nosworthy, London, 1997)

Wilson, Sir Robert, *Brief Remarks on the Character and Composition of the Russian Army* (London, 1810)

Wood, Sir Evelyn, *Cavalry in the Waterloo Campaign* (London, 1895)

Wood, Sir Evelyn, *Achievements of Cavalry* (London, 1897)

SOURCE NOTES

(1) Rocca, A.J.M. de, *Memoirs of the War of the French in Spain* (London, r/p 1990), pp 72–73

(2) Maxwell, Sir Herbert, *The Life of Wellington* (London, 1899), Vol II pp 138–39

(3) Brack, A.F. de, *Light Cavalry Outposts* (London, 1876), p xiii

(4) Marbot, J.B.A.M. (trans. A.J. Butler), *The Memoirs of Baron de Marbot* (London, 1913), Vol I, p 34

(5) Rocca, p 73

(6) Roberts, D., *The Military Adventures of Johnny Newcome* (London, 1816), p 189

(7) Gleig, Revd. G.R., *The Subaltern* (Edinburgh & London, 1872), pp 270–71

(8) Ker Porter, R., *Letters from Portugal and Spain* (pub. under nom-de-plume 'An Officer', London, 1809), pp 218–19

(9) Tomkinson, W. (ed. J. Tomkinson), *The Diary of a Cavalry Officer in the Peninsula and Waterloo Campaigns* (London, 1895), p 159

(10) Cotton, E., *A Voice from Waterloo* (9th edn, Brussels, 1900), p 260

(11) Tomkinson, p 101

(12) *United Service Journal* (hereafter *USJ*) 1840, Vol III, pp 525–26

(13) Marbot, Vol II, pp 628–29

(14) Leeke, Revd. W., *Supplement to the History of Lord Seaton's Regiment ... at the Battle of Waterloo* (London, 1871), pp 56–57

(15) *USJ* 1831, Vol II, p 73

(16) Marbot, Vol II, pp 538–39

(17) Tomkinson, pp 115–16

(18) Swabey, W. (ed. F.A. Whinyates), *Diary of Campaigns in the Peninsula...* (Woolwich, 1895; London edn, 1984), p 114

(19) This and following quotations from Wilson, *Brief Remarks...* (London, 1810), pp 26–33

(20) Labaume, E., *A Circumstantial Narrative of the Campaign in Russia* (London, 1814), p 121

(21) Marbot, Vol II, pp 645–46

(22) Tomkinson, p 35

(23) *The Times*, 22 June 1815

(24) Kincaid, Sir John, *Adventures in the Rifle Brigade*, and *Random Shots from a Rifleman* (combined edn, London, 1908), p 234

(25) This translation from *Edinburgh Evening Courant*, 7 September 1793

(26) *USJ* 1831, Vol II, p 75

(27) Mercer, Gen. A.C., *Journal of the Waterloo Campaign* (Edinburgh & London, 1870), Vol I, p 279

(28) *USJ* 1840, Vol III, p 32

(29) *British Military Library or Journal* (London, 1798), Vol I, p 139

(30) Tomkinson, pp 5–6

(31) Gordon, A. (ed. H.C. Wylly), *A Cavalry Officer in the Corunna Campaign 1808–09* (London, 1913), p 102

(32) Gordon, p 107

INDEX